Amphipolitan

Skirting the transient city

A poetry collection by

Emmylou Kotzé

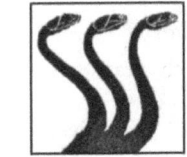

PINK HYDRA PRESS
2024

Copyright

Amphipolitan: Skirting the transient city

© 2019, 2024 Emmylou Kotzé

amphipolitan.com; email emmyktz@amphipolitan.com

Pink Hydra Press

thepinkhydra.com; email submissions@thepinkhydra.com

Pink Hydra edition 7 May 2024

Paperback: 978-0-7961-7354-6

e-book: 978-0-7961-7355-3

SOME RIGHTS RESERVED. The text and cover art of this book are licensed under the Creative Commons Attribution-NonCommercial-NoDerivatives 4.0 International License. To view a copy of this license, visit http://creativecommons.org/licenses/by-nc-nd/4.0/ or send a letter to Creative Commons, PO Box 1866, Mountain View, CA 94042, USA. The work may be shared and redistributed in any format as long as attribution is given and it is not used for commercial purposes. If you remix, transform, or build upon the material, you may not distribute the modified material. For commercial distribution, please contact the author.

All illustrations used in the interior of this work are in the public domain, or intellectual property rights have been waived to their fullest extent so that they may be shared, modified or redistributed without any restrictions. Original sources of images, where known, are provided in the back of the book.

Although this book has been inspired by the events of the author's life, any reference or allusion to real-life people or events has either been invented, exaggerated, or used metaphorically. No reference to any real person or event is meant as a faithful or truthful representation, but only as the author's own flight of fancy.

LIST OF POEMS

I.	Supernova	1
II.	Dark Sorceress	3
III.	Dominus Mortis	4
IV.	Venus	6
V.	Five	7
VI.	In A Box	13
VII.	Charge Me	14
VIII.	The Cheater	15
IX.	Selfish Love	16
X.	Glory Be	17
XI.	The Eternal Dirge	19
XII.	Vs. Order	20
XIII.	Encounter	21
XIV.	Walk This Way	24
XV.	Asterix	25
XVI.	The Bottle and the Body	29
XVII.	Children of the World	30
XVIII.	The Fate of Linden	31

XIX.	Thoughts on An Estranged Lover While Fixing Morning Coffee	38
XX.	The Lost Cat	39
XXI.	Finale Smith	40
XXII.	She Crouches on A Rocky Floor	43
XXIII.	Days of Romance, Days of Yore	46
XXIV.	The Weary Traveller	50
XXV.	Witches' Hollow	55
XXVI.	Night-Time	60
XXVII.	Another Brick in the Wall	62
XXVIII.	On the Discovery of Winter	63
XXIX.	Sleep	64
XXX.	The Minor Gods	66
XXXI.	Limitless	67
XXXII.	Stars	67
XXXIII.	Springtime	71
XXXIV.	The Wizard	72
XXXV.	The Spell	80
XXXVI.	Black Ribbon	84
XXXVII.	Guns	86
XXXVIII.	Hitman	89

XXXIX.	Mary Jane	91
XL.	Mia	92
XLI.	The Student's Plea to Minerva	93
XLII.	The Fantasy	94
XLIII.	The Hero Within	98
XLIV.	Home	102
XLV.	To A Dead Swallow by the Side of the Road	105
XLVI.	Polyhymnia	107
XLVII.	The Cracked Mirror	112
XLVIII.	It Feels Like Freedom	113
XLIX.	Aimlessly Looking For My Love	116
L.	To Any University, Anywhere on Earth	118
LI.	Timeless	120
LII.	The Naming of Stephen Rae	122
LIII.	The Curse of Lara Twilight	125
LIV.	Relating To Lorna Doone	132
LV.	The Ballad-Tale of Vaila Lana	133
LVI.	Rietta	141
LVII.	Oh What Are You Doing, and Where Are You Going?	145

LVIII.	At Last! A Bit of Peace and Quiet!	148
LIX.	The Guarded Heart	149
LX.	Storm	156
LXI.	Butterfly Far Beyond Willow Trees	157
LXII.	O Lovely Rose	159
LXIII.	The Vampyre Queen	160
LXIV.	The Mines	183
LXV.	The People	187
LXVI.	A Hair	189
LXVII.	Blue Nation	192
LXVIII.	Sister Softly Sleeping	195
LXIX.	Call To Troy	201
LXX.	The Lament of the Elves For Their Dead Warriors	202
LXXI.	The Winner	205
LXXII.	Werewolf Song: Nightshade and Harp	207
LXXIII.	Claws	210
LXXIV.	Reasons You Shouldn't Leave	211
LXXV.	Farewell	216
LXXVI.	The Night Is Beautiful	217
LXXVII.	Peggy May of the North Country	218

LXXVIII.	Frozen Road	222
LXXIX.	Fair Are the Brides	225
LXXX.	In the City Where the Rain Still Falls	229
LXXXI.	Eldertree	231
LXXXII.	Winteraand op die Hoëveld/ Winter's Night on the Highveld	232
LXXXIII.	The Visitor	235
LXXXIV.	The Years	237

'Elaine the fair, Elaine the loveable,
Elaine, the lily maid of Astolat—'

—Alfred, Lord Tennyson, *Lancelot and Elaine*

'The question, so frequently asked me—"How I, then a young girl, came to think of, and to dilate upon, so very hideous an idea?"'

—Mary Shelley, *1831 Introduction to Frankenstein*

'Was this the face that launched a thousand ships,
And burned the topless towers of Ilium?—
Sweet Helen, make me immortal with a kiss!'

—Christopher Marlowe, *The Tragical History of Doctor Faustus*

'I think that is the saddest thing that ever happens in this world, when women pass through great suffering that makes them become as men.'

—Herman Charles Bosman, *The Rooinek*

FOREWORD

It is a natural human inclination to seek to define oneself by finding models in the world around us and society. From a very young age, I have sought to define myself through the literature I perused, through the books I read and the television shows I watched.

Amphipolis is a historical Athenian settlement in Thrace, a stronghold at the outskirts of Greek civilization, settled between the mountains and the sea. It is also the home of the fictional warrior princess, Xena.

Us modern women would like to see ourselves as Xenas: strong, beautiful and in control of our own destinies. But the women whose stories and contemplations may be found in this book are not like that. They are weaker, and more insecure.

In my life, deny it as I might, I have found more in common with the women who prevaricate, who weep, who follow their men everywhere. With the Elaines, who felt that their only certain way out of misery was death; with the Helens, pawns of mightier players who held the power of life and happiness over them; with the unnamed love interests and titillators who only exist on the fringes of storytelling. This book represents my years of wandering through their world, struggling to find my place. Trying to define how the chroniclers of the future might write about me.

Most of the poems in this book are either romantic, tragic or both. They are often written in archaic language, evoking a sense of the past to bring the people of bygone eras into our present day. Sometimes, they merely dream of simpler worlds, transient realities and the magic that is inherent to all poetry.

This book is dedicated to the women who could never be strong, who were never heroines. Weakness does not equate with worthlessness, and without questioning, poetry would not exist. Where the contemplations of civilization meet the untamed wilderness, in the crook of the mountains beside the sea, around the transient city, there our poetry may be found.

AMPHIPOLITAN
SKIRTING THE TRANSIENT CITY

I

SUPERNOVA

A War Song

All the evil has already been
and we build our foundations, not of stone
but of blood, pain and suffering.
People have died.
Chances have died,
but we are the future.

In the past, the battle is over
as it starts a new beginning.
Is the war already won?
Our time will pass.

Our joy will pass,
but we are the future.

Do you hear the war-drums beating again?
Prepare for the new last battle.
Prepare for the fight that never ends.
Battles will fail.
Plans will fail,
but we are the future.

And we must disgorge the doubt in our hearts
and strive on heedless of foe;
and all things fair that the world once knew
we seek to redeem and regrow.
We have seen great structures, kingdoms, fall;
and we know that many more must perish
before we strike back, and strike down evil,
and at last our goal of freedom is reached.
Many will live.
Many will die,
but we are the future.

II

DARK SORCERESS

Dark Sorceress,
with robes of sacred power,
sigils of life and death.
The gods shiver when they see you;
all men bow down before you;
you are their deity,
Dark Sorceress.

Princess of the Night,
beasts shy away from you,
men flee before you.
Vengeful wraiths rise up for you,
kings prepare victims for you;
you are their ruler,
Princess of the Night.

Bringer of War,
whose voice commands mountains,

whose voice commands awe.
Fearful are warriors of you,
chieftains lay their swords before you;
you are their mistress,
Bringer of War.

Dark Sorceress,
you are feared in life and even in death.
Upon the wings of evil
there sits a princess;
there sits a killer;
there sits a goddess,
Dark Sorceress.

III

DOMINUS MORTIS

He walks alone; he walks among
the graves of all the joy he's known,
and though he'd pause, prayers murmuring,

no earthly comfort comes to him;
he walks alone, he walks in dread.
His wife watches, tears a-falling;
doesn't hear the dying calling
out to him, in his head screaming,
like goblins from witched dreaming:
not real to him, they're only dead.
But ever he must see their suffering faces
deep in his dark empty open spaces,
telling him, 'Never shall we lie to rest;
evermore do you feel us in your fatherly breast;
we are the ones who rule and ruin—
O Dominus Mortis! One who cannot mourn!
Carry us on, Lord: be not forsaking;
for crimes to the Dead are sure sins in the making!'
Ever they call, but he never replies;
one who speaks with the dead is surely not wise!
Yet they call him before the dew sets on the grass
and he gnaws down and hopes that their voices
    will pass—
He walks alone and he walks with the dead.

IV

VENUS

    She waits alone.
Mourning the names of daughters killed,
Their words of rebellion brutally stilled
    In the deathlight spreading over seas.

    She waits alone,
Wrapped in colours wonderful
In the dying twilight beautiful,
    A wonder that Man no more sees.

    She sways alone,
Knowing her beauty a silent victim,
Symbol of peace now propagating
    mayhem—
    A Mother Earth that no-one needs.

V

FIVE

A Romance of Bloemfontein

Here's an epic tale told of heroes;
brave were they, and five in number:
three were feline, two, canine,
but none with selfishness encumbered.
They had a Mistress, but she oft was gone
to humanly pursuits one cannot guess—
Hunting for food?—
But the minute she left

Out they came; and they were no longer
dog or cat, nor pet or familiar;
five were they in number:
Tessie of the White Paws, compassionate
to any creature that ever walked this earth;
Charlie, her sidekick, the Pint-Sized-Pest;
dapper was he, and bold as a falcon.
Omit not the cats: Big Billy and his mother;

Su Lin she was called, the name of a queen
who had married for love.
Last but not least, the black one, the sleek one,
Moxlet the foxy cat, mistress of shadows;
soft was her fur and low was her purr,
sweet to the ears, oh: all would concur!

These five, they had their adventures in dozens,
hundreds, even: they were heroes of the cause!
Let a kitten chip its nail, or a dog hurt its paw;
an Afghan into burrs, a terrier into thorn,
the five were on duty: they'd never hesitate
to step to a good cause when it awaited.
Once, even, they rescued a mouse from a horse;
the little rodent had got stuck in one of its hoofs
as the clumsy beast had charged over the plain
heeding none in its trot over the dry, parched terrain!
It took many hours; it took many claws,
but the five were victorious: the mouse was free!
To be a bit more careful of great horse-paws,
lest scooped up again and dragged into a stall!

Most days in the land of the Five were windy,
dry and hot, sometimes stuffy too;
but there came a day in the middle of January,
when it rained and rained; all the clouds were full!
It was not a day one would have liked to be out;
the forceful precipitation might be welcome after
    drought
but the streets and pavements were flooded with the
    rain!
The five were inside resting; they wished not to be wet;
even Tessie, wisest, gentlest, on the warm dry bed did
    sit;
but then they heard
the sharp anguish of a bird
who has something to tell that cannot wait.

Charlie he ran outside; he wished to ask the bird,
'Why are you not in your nest? What evil have you
    heard?'
But he saw a little figure, far off, drenched in the rain;
its little mouth was open; it meowed a scream of pain.
Charlie bolder than falcon ran and ran till he found Bill:

'There is a kitten in the far street! What is there to do?'
Said Bill: 'We cannot go there; the far street is
    forbidden.
A wise cat does not tarry there; it belongs to the
    machines.
No-one will attempt to cross it, so many have been
    flattened;
we cannot go there, puppy: the far street is forbidden.'
But Charlie he was obstinate: he called the Five
    together:
'O valiant heroes, listen! An animal's in danger!
Lying drenched in the far street, that place of abject
    terror;
let us plan its rescue, friends! let's not sit here warm
and dry, while a lonely creature dies in the storm.'

The five they laid a plan, formed a rescue party,
ventured out into the storm, protected by an old
sheet that they had found in the room of their Mistress.
Not even Billy the doubter dared
to question their bold quest,

for some things are more important than human-
    induced distress.
They arrived at the far street; it resembled a river,
but Tessie was not scared; she splashed out to the kitten;
Big Billy and Su Lin rode on her back—
Meanwhile, Moxie, the small one, the sleek one,
crept to one end of the road to act as a lookout
while Charlie did the same at the other end.

Billy and his mama hooked the kit on Tessie's back,
prepared to leave the accursed place;
but Mox screamed warning: 'a car's a-coming!
Run, my dear ones, Tessie, run!'
But the current was too strong; Tessie couldn't move,
the cats on her back screamed blue murder—
the car approached, headlights blazing—
but then the current started moving—
The current washed dear Tess away; away from evil
    death!
Spluttering, Tess swam strongly—clambered to the
    pavement,
drenched and tired, very wet, but gloriously alive!

The heroes returned to Headquarters, dried the kitten well,
saved another life again; were even more renowned,
for they'll brave any evil, be it high water or hell,
manmade cruelty and neglect, injury and pain;
Tessie of the White Paws, Moxlet, Billy, Suse
and Charlie the little Pint-Sized Pest: Heroes Of The Cause!
Not for little are they known as Gallant Five today;
rely on them to save the kingdom: Heroes Of Today!

VI

IN A BOX

As the hobo said to the stray cat

Me, human,
You, feline,
Locked in a box so sublime, so sublime,
Like abandoned socks—
I know I've abandoned mine.
It's rain, feline;
Rain in this box.
Soaking your fur so divine, so divine;
Sleet in a box,
and snow in a mine.

Me, human,
You, feline;
Sheltered in a box.

VII

CHARGE ME

Charge me
like I were a cellphone and you,
you were my battery;
sweeten me
like you were the sugar and I,
I were the tea.
But if you were carbon I'd be arsenic
to poison you;
and if you were potassium I'd be the proton
to destabilize you;
as we chase around in circles like electrons,
delicate figures-of-eight,
let me be frank:
Stab me,
like you were a soldier and I,
I were your enemy.

VIII

THE CHEATER

I knocked at the door,
Stooped by absolution;
You sat up straight from kneeling,
    resenting the intrusion.
    I think of you no more:—
Oh, who am I trying to kid?
I ponder all the lies and schemes behind
    this mask you hid.
    You should have suffered more,
Have suffered like I do,
As corrupted and deceitful became the
    love I knew.

> Don't think of me as 'poor';
> Don't pity me at all;
> I've always been as I am now, my back
> > against the wall.
> > I wish you happiness;
> — Don't speak or think of me;
> Don't dark my door no more, darling—it's
> > locked and you've no key.

IX

SELFISH LOVE

> These boots of love for thee I wore,
> > But let my burden not be shown;
> In these trials for thee I bore,
> > I worked and walked this road alone.
> But thou didst stray so far from me,
> > That, end in end, we'd be apart;
> With what wouldst thou lay *this* on me?
> > What selfish love? what broken heart?

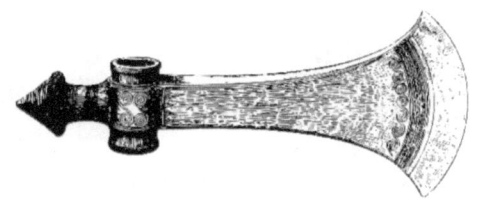

X

GLORY BE

   Glory be,
The Lord has hacked up my enemy
   And thrown him here,
Entrails gutted, for all to see.
   The glory is mine:
Who waded in his blood? Who laughed as he died?
   I turn away
From the widow's wailing and the children's crying.

Angels sing;
They serenade the fall of all worldly things.
I jeer at you:
You who were fool enough to cherish my ring.
The glory is mine:
I bathed in your blood. I laughed as you died.
What are you,
But a pathetic bundle of pleading and crying?

Monstrous are You,
Training me since birth to become a killer true.
But soon you will see,
Strong am I, and in time I will taste your blood too.
You can try:
Strike me down with thunder, and make this seem a lie,
But I am quick;
Strike me down with thunder now, and sooner will You die.

XI

THE ETERNAL DIRGE

His vibrant colour, laced with pearl,
    That face that caused maidens to weep,
And eyes with darkened lashes furled,
    Seemed unfit for eternal sleep;
But yet, so soon his earthly joys
    Have gone to death and darkened deep:—
They writ his grave: 'Here lies a boy—
    The world to release, God to keep.'

Tick on, tick on, Eternal Clock!
    Count you each tortured, burning breath,
'Til we all sleep 'neath casque and lock,
    And reach the final goal—to Death!
Weep, ye maidens! full well you may,
    For him who takes a draught of Lethe,
To wash this life, this ache, away,
    And know only this gentle Death!

XII

VS. ORDER

My inspiration came from grass lush enough to be forest
    to an army of ants
my inspiration came from the green furriness of an
    aniseed plant
my inspiration came from the sanctuary of a shadow
    cast by a tree
my inspiration came from the candy-pink four-p.m
    flowers, ugly enough to be weeds, yet the most
    beautiful plants I'll ever see.
But no more
You came, your words spoke of mush and mud
stalks of churned dead grasses spurted up like blood
you uprooted my trees, you tore my flowers away
Why do I even write any longer?
It's always been all about you anyway
Where my weeds once were I see flowerbeds,
empty, mud-filled flowerbeds.

XIII

ENCOUNTER

'Miss me?' he says;
  Confidently
He strides over
  — To excite me!

'Miss me?' he says;
  Grins stupidly;
Eyes mischievous,
  Hair all messy!

'Miss me?' he says;
  Daydreams awake;
Was I asleep?
  Smile for his sake!

'Miss me?' he says;
  Eyes soft and brown—
Love, don't catch me!

Let me fall down!

'Miss me?' he says;
   Kneels on the floor;
I was lonely...
   Not now! no more!

'Love me,' he says;
   Confidently
His body moves
   — To excite me!

'Love me,' he says;
   Grins stupidly;
No barriers—
   Hair all messy!

'Love me,' he says;
   Daydreams awake;
Don't dream too much—
   Smile for his sake!

'Love me,' he says;
  Eyes soft and brown—
Love, in their depths,
  Let me fall down!

'Love me,' he says;
  Kneels on the floor;
No turning back;
  Not now! no more!

XIV

WALK THIS WAY

Well, I was walking to the shop on a beautiful day;
    It was a morn, a frosty morn;
And up to me came a fine lady all prim and tight
    On that morn, that frosty morn.
And she said: 'Put your chin up! put your head down!
    There's no excuse to walk like you do!
Stop your slouching! put your shoulders high!
    Remember to walk this way!'

Now I was ambling along all looking for fun,
    One afternoon, an afternoon,
And there was a little girl looking up at me
    In the afternoon, the afternoon.
And she said: 'Put your chin up! put your head down!
    You gotta walk the correct way!
Stop your slouching! put your shoulders high!
    My mommy told me to walk this way!'

So I was strolling along going back to my home
  In the night, one dark night,
And I espied a beggar sitting up on his rags
  In the night, in the dark night.
And he said: 'Put your chin up! put your head down!
  It's a question of honour, you know!
Stop your slouching! put your shoulders high!
  In wartime we walk this way!'

XV

ASTERIX

So here we are, *Asterix*. I'd name a star for you;
Now that you've had your look at me d'you think we'd
  make it through?
Would you take me speeding through the night like a
  superman of stars,
When my blood's pumping caffeine and pretty boys in
  cars?
I've never seen you passionate; I've not seen you at all,

but with your quirky words and teasing wit you held
these blue eyes in thrall!
I wished we were alone, so I could see you at unease,
and our roles would then turn round and I'd be the one
with tease—
I'm not wearing my blue eyeliner for nothing now, you
know:
Neither my corset top! and I wish you'd let something
show!—
Too cool, too fine, too humorous: is this you or your
façade?
When you texted me last night I thought our fairytale'd
be made!—
Asterix, light in the sky, master of the comic smile,
Do you lose interest quickly, or does flirtation take a
while?
Don't you try and play hard to get; you're good at being
good;
Can a good boy come all over strange and resort to
being crude?
I lit a match and thought of you, so bright before you
fade

In significance, and so I knew—all only a charade;
Question is: why then and there, and why ever at all?
Did my burnished image fade to you, like fireworks to the fall?
I give you up, and smile sadly, for *Asterix*, my star—
Perhaps someday we'll level then, in heaven where you are—
And you'll apologize for dreams, for high heels and corsets;
You'll say the reason why and I know I will accept it;
Till then, till then, my *Asterix*, look bright in my dark sky,
And far away, and far from me, and never tell me why!
Take my dreams, and caffeine, and pretty boys in cars,
And take them far away from me, among the outer stars!
And take you too my rhapsodies of supermen in space,
And cast my eyes to search among the men of earthly race;
Remind me so, my dying star, perfection's not extant!
For you're not perfect, *Asterix*, but you're my star and saint!

Remind me of the fancies of a sixteen-year-old girl:
The beauty sipping coffee, dressed in fishnet tights and pearls—
Goodbye, my love—adieu—I wish we could have been closer,
But once again, my *Asterix*, I am the clear loser!
What might have been? what might have been? indeed, but just remind
Me of pretty boys, and caffeine, and gods among mankind!

XVI

THE BOTTLE AND THE BODY

In the central square of Bloemfontein there lies a bottle
an unbroken bottle
an empty, unbroken bottle of Smirnoffs' Spin.

In the donga near the central square there lies a body
a body blue and throttled
an empty, broken body dead and throttled.

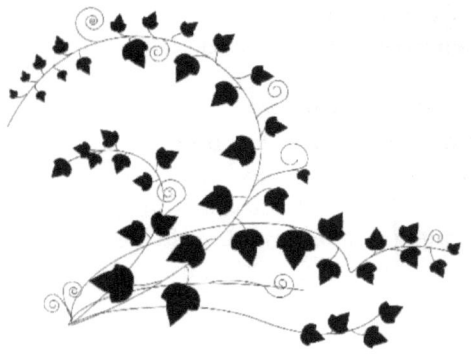

XVII

CHILDREN OF THE WORLD

Children of the world, unite!
Though guns cry out and cannons ring;
Though, standing 'round us, people die;
Though songs of blood—revolt, they sing,
Will we stand up, reject the lie?

Children of the world, unite!
Blazing dynamite and bombs
Have marred our past and sealed our fate
And paved our way to deathly tombs;
If you want peace, you're born too late!

Children of the world, unite!
The march begins, the march of truth;
Their words we fight, their wars we fell,
Though bound from birth and quashed in youth;
Though born in gunfire, raised in Hell!

Children of the world, unite!
The march begins, the march of truth;
Born of the world, we march to Hell
To crack its walls and raise its roof
With echoes of the tales we tell!

Children of the world, no thanks
Do we owe to the blighting world;
Cast off your chains and free your feet;
Fear *us* they should—not we the world;
We march as leaders, not as slaves;
We march with Truth to free the world;
They should fear us—we've the power—
March with Truth—to wreak the world!

XVIII

THE FATE OF LINDEN

This is the town that we live in:
Muddy and ragged and grey;

The rain never gives in, the clouds never flee,
The demon-mist never gives way.
Yet there's a tale, told by grandmothers hale,
That it was not always thus:
The mists were not here; the sunlight shone clear;
No lupine wailing was heard at midnight,
The night-stars shone bright, no evil in sight;
We were happy, the old people say.
Our unkempt main street was cobbled and neat;
If you would've cared to ride
At a dead gallop through our wide city streets,
Oh, you'd never have wanted to hide!
For cheerful were all, and coloured the stalls
That now are a wolfish grey,
And for miles you could hear the cries and the cheers—
We were happy, the old people say.

In that time, in the frosty month of November,
A wedding was planned:
'Twas to be the one great event to remember
Not only in town, but all over the land!
The bride was our Mary, child of a knight;

Her father had honour, and valour bright;
Her mother was fair, and a servant of Light.
As for Mary herself—no horrid blight
Was seen in her face, was heard in her voice,
Was felt in her deeds,
Was found in her prayers; for, when given a choice,
She'd pray for the poor, and help those in need.
As befitted a maid of her stature and wealth
She took no yokel as man—the Prince himself
Had courted her favour, and now, as is good,
Was to wed her in our little kirk in the woods!

The day of the wedding dawned perfect—the sun
Out of the clouds did shine his face,
And bathe the bride in colours of sunsets,
Resplendent in lace
And silk—all white,
In the woods, like an angel about to take flight.
All said that the grace of the Lord had shone
On the wedding, and surely'd continue on;
The bride stood ready to take her walk in,
How lovely she looked! the guests were whispering;

The trees stood bare—no wind was blowing;
Behind their branches the sunshine was glowing;
How lovely looked she!
But wait! a cloud slips over the sun,
A cloud so thick, so dense, and so grey,
It kills the rays that have lit the scene—
As all looked up, the light died away!

From the air a flapping of wings was heard,
And a shadow so black came swooping down,
So dark and so dread, that half the guests fled,
Ere the alien creature had reached the ground!
A split second more, and a shape was seen;
There were wings! there were fangs! how everyone
    screamed,
As the spectre pounced with a smile obscene,
As inch-long fangs in the daylight gleamed!

And all at that moment swore
That they had seen airborne Death:
For a coldness swept over the kirk:
A cold that dampened the breath.

Everyone fled for the kirk,
Cowering coldly inside,
All that were present that day,
Everyone save for the bride,
Who was trapped by a cloud of smoke,
'Til somebody realized—
Shouted the Prince: 'Let me out! What if she has died?'

Oh, that the groom had been right!
Oh, that fair Mary had died that morrow!
But this Death, who out from the skies
Had risen with winds of impending sorrow,
Stepped unto her, and said thus:
'Fair maiden, I see perfection!
Would that you were mine;
Would that I were your groom,
Receiving your hand for all time!'
And then that creature swept the girl
Off the ground, with a wind that whirls,
And the wedding-guests clustered all around
And stared up high, above the ground,
Where all around them, the whirlwind sang,

As into her throat he sank his fangs;
She fell unconscious; the crowd were still,
Silent from the horror that every mind filled—
With a grin in farewell, the spectre left,
Left the groom staring, of all bereft,
And the coldness lifted, but stormclouds brewing
Were left, and a hail of icicles blew in.
All that of Mary was found
Was a slipper, one slipper, of white;
And this was placed in the kirk
As the ice-storm sang and blew through the night.

Oh, what a hateful tragedy!
How the merry groom did mourn!
And though for months they searched and searched,
Never was she found—no creature did burn;
And, as if in sympathy
For the father's grief, our lovely Sun
Hid his face behind the clouds,
And still, when so many days have run,
Never have we seen Him since;
The clouds are here, the mist is hence!

The trees are bare, the crops don't grow;
The children weep, their hearts in woe;
A curse so cruel on Linden-town
The spectre that fateful day did lease;
O mourning town! O ragged town!
How drear and bare are all your trees!
All our colours fade to grey;
All the tears we weep, in vain;
Perhaps will come a glorious day,
A time for which our preachers pray,
When our crops shall grow and our children play!
But 'til then we lie dreary,
Wintry and weary,
Mourning a virgin's fate!—
They say our salvation
Lies in prayer and conviction,
But oh! too late! too late!

XIX

THOUGHTS ON AN ESTRANGED LOVER WHILE FIXING MORNING COFFEE

you came into the kitchen
you loomed like an eyesore
against my five-foot figure
and the two-metre door

and I made you coffee
I like it strong and black
and you turned off the light
and you never came back

I'm in my kitchen now
my coffee before my
baggy eyes and robbed lips;
Why? Asterix, tell me why?

XX

THE LOST CAT

I once had a little black cat,
   So pretty, always neat as a pin,
With silky-soft fur on her back,
And little padding paws on a track,
   And eyes as yellow as sin.

I lost my pretty black cat,
   And I know not where she lies.
Not of the tomb that binds her,
Nor of the lands where I shall find her,
   Not even whe'er she lives or she's died.

XXI

FINALE SMITH

Finale Smith
was a city-gutter girl;
she lived in the slum,
she wanted the world.
She dreamt by night
and sometimes by day;
oftentimes we would hear
Master Johnson say:
'Pay attention to me,
Finale Smith!'

Finale Smith
had a face so fair
that you'd pay just to see

and stare, and stare;
and often, at break,
all the boys hung about,
not one of them voicing
what they wanted to shout:
'Pay attention to me,
Finale Smith!'

Finale Smith
was a secretive girl:
she never shared her all
with any in the world,
but she talked and wrote
and her tales could woo;
was as if every pen
and paper said, too:
'Pay attention to me,
Finale Smith!'

Finale Smith
left home at sixteen;
she rented a flat,

worked at a canteen;
her grades were top,
but her house a mess;
you could *hear* the rooms
all pleading in distress:
'Pay attention to us,
Finale Smith!'

Finale Smith
was the talk of the school:
Head Girl to boot
and no Euclid's fool;
all wished for her brain,
but not for her head,
for she seldom listened
when Authority said:
'Pay attention to me,
Finale Smith!'

Finale Smith
is nowhere to be found:
she left our country

for greener grounds.
In faraway seas
she is roaming about,
but can't stay for long,
for every land shouts:
'Pay a visit to me,
Finale Smith;
pay attention to me,
Finale Smith!'

XXII

SHE CROUCHES ON A ROCKY FLOOR

She crouches on a rocky floor;
The noisome reek of damp creeps o'er
The hole she hides in—mouldy crack
With dying, stagnant water black;
She holds her breath—wishes away
The bright, intruding searchlight's ray;
The crumbling mountain moans and roars,

But through it all,
She's suffered more.

Bright, gentle maidens 'round her wove,
Young orphans in her kitchens throve;
Her halls were decked in marigolds,
Her merry dress, with pink and gold;
When passing here, one would witness
Love, wisdom, hope, and happiness;
A vernal arch aflown with doves,
    Which, with it all,
    She'd dearly love.

A selfish monarch claimed the throne,
And swore a vow her will to own,
But swore another in its place
When she refused all his false grace;
He spurned her words as blasphemy,
Her companions as heresy,
And in his dungeons had her thrown,

So, through it all,
She'd be alone.

The hangman bleak and faceless stood;
Within the rope, the lady good;
Three times they pushed her—all in vain;
Three times the hang-rope snapped in twain;
For her the townsfolk made the cry:
'The Lord's beloved cannot die!'
The king with thwarted ire stood,
And, through it all,
Ne'er understood.

She fled the whip and cruel hounds,
All frozen, hurting, danger-bound;
Ran through the forest—reached the hill,
Fled man and beast both crazed to kill,
And sought to find the land of Light,
Where dark be day and wrongs be right,
And healing lay for every wound,
But, through it all,
She never found.

She crouches in the cave so still,
Peering through mists that haunt the hill;
Exile will be her only fate—
Forever hiding from the hate
Of one who cannot understand
The wealth of love and trusting hands;
Through all her tears the cave is still,
    But give life up—
    She never will.

XXIII

DAYS OF ROMANCE, DAYS OF YORE

Now our world eclipses beauty;
Now we plod, laden with duty;

Take a trip and ride with me,

Till we come to the Northern Sea;

Then fashion me a sailing-boat,
And way up north, to ice, we'll float,

But I am weak and can't go far,
So follow me the Northern Star;

Find the Pole and cut the slack,
And bring the Past all rolling back;

Give me romance, bring me glory,
Find the poets, sing their stories;

Bring me myth and tale and creed,
And give me heart and word and deed;

Pile the hearth with logs a-laden,
Sing of lake and river-maiden;

Give me golden swords and dragons,
Ebon halls and blazing flagons;

Give me gallants young and gay,
And let the harp and lyre play,

And let the children, barefoot, run,
And dance in cowslips 'neath the sun;

O give me gentle summer rain,
And high, diamond-shaped windowpanes;

O set me on the lonely isles,
Where forests stretch for miles and miles;

Then take me to the Alpine woods,
And wrap me in a doeskin hood;

O set me on the cliffs of rock,
Where waves the land for ever mock,

And amber lines the stony shore,
A remnant washed from years of yore;

O bring me to the castles proud,
And show me kings with holy shrouds,

And damsels fair and wise and true,
And warriors all painted blue,

And heroes riding to the dawn,
And wise goatherds with staff and horn,

And honest farmers working well,
And forest-witches weaving spells;

O bring me longbow, sabre, spear,
To make this city disappear;

O bring me magic, potions, charms,
To summon all the Past to arms;

Awake the goblin, fairy, sprite;
They'll lift this cloud of mortal spite;

O find the Pole and cut that slack,
And bring the Past all rolling back;

O find me all the ruins that lie
Of times that were—and had to die!

XXIV

THE WEARY TRAVELLER

'Come hither, weary traveller:
    No comfort will you find
In your dust and gravel here,
    With your home so far behind.
Why brays your ass a weary might?
    Why drag your feet along?
What missive be yours, dreary wight,
    That you hum this dirge along?
Were you once merry, in your home,
    Beyond a far far sea?'

'Beyond the hill, beyond a stone,
    There lies the land of the free!
Away, away from present woes
    A path winds up a hill,
Leading to a beach where the thrashing throes
    Of the sea lie ever still.
Upon this beach, there is a cove
    Of granite white and grey;
Here seaweed sings, and cockles cleave,
    And anemones sway.
Here, fish dance in the seething swells
    And fry play in their midst;
Sea-slugs, eels, and cockle-shells
    Bathe together in watery tryst.
And here, echoing against the rocks,
    A song of surf and sea,
Of sinking ships, and dying docks,
    And fishes swimming free,
Reverberates ever near and far,
    And bubbling sorrow grows,
And becomes broken, bleeding scars,
    All of what mankind owes.

This lamentation grows so strong
    That if you stand, you die;
Thus Mermen lament all the wrongs
    Bedone by humankind.
Their dwelling there, below the waves,
    Is calm and clean and cool;
No war rages, no tyrant raves;
    Their monarch is not cruel.
His palace is of ice-crystal;
    His beard is long and white;
A wise man he, but sure able
    To scare rogues into flight.
His people, they are bright and gay;
    Their songs, they line the streets,
And, Rider, O! on festal days,
    A merry lot you'll meet!
The King rides in a sea-carriage,
    Decked in coral and gold;
Dancing fish line his passage,
    Their mail silver and cold.
The Mermaidens, with sparkling hair,
    Wearing true oyster-pearls,

Sway the world from its weary cares
    With a twist and a turn and a swirl.
Happy, happy beneath the world,
    A sailor's dream alive;
Twisting whirlpools, burnished bodies,
    Joyfully wild and lithe!'

'So does this weary traveller
    Come wandering from sea?'

'Yea, this poor grey dirt-groveler
    With a tired-out donkey
Comes with the dear recollection
    Of a merry, merry home;
A home that rides all directions
    In the hollow, heaving foam.
O dear kingdom! O naked dreams!
    Would that I were back there!
This Earth-existence arid seems
    Compared to the Ocean dear!
O claim me back, you mournful waves!
    See my melancholy!

Is there a grace which sinners saves
   From their tortured Eternity?
I will die here; of that I'm sure,
   Broken, banished, and alone,
Thinking on all the things that were
   Among the things I own:
A worn-out ass, a travel-pack,
   A fond, sad memory,
Half a penny, an ancient track
   Trod by all and sundry;
A conscience fit to mar all wit,
   The guilt of deeds a-done;
Here, now, looking back at it,
   I know why I was shunned!
O tragic times! O wrongful sin!
   Rider, beyond that stone,
Beyond that track, O there you'll win
   The deep-blue land of home!
Beyond the beach, beyond that cove,
   Where mermaids swim and sing—
O Rider, yea, the land I love
   Is far, oh so far from this poor inn!'

XXV

WITCHES' HOLLOW

The sun was light and ponds were shallow,
The morning dawned bright in Witches' Hollow.
The wind whispered; trees sighed by the stream,
Calling all near to join the daydream.
The stately old crone stepped out of her hut,
A straw-thatched roof, with a floor all of mud;
She leaned on her stick and whispered her prayer:
She revered the Seven Sisters of the Isle of the Mare.
And though her lips drooled and her jaw hung slack,
Alas to the fiend who'd target her back!
    There was life again in the land of shadow;
    The sun awakened in Witches' Hollow.

The sun glittered off the drops of the Stream of Sorrows;
The stream flowed down into Witches' Hollow.
She walked beside the water dressed all in black:
Poor peasant girl but no grace did she lack.
She walked in awareness of a sacred power;

She'd pray when the clock struck the midnight hour;
She had grey-blue eyes and icy blonde hair,
Like the people who served on the Isle of the Mare.
There lay her reverence: the Isle and its sacred Art;
It flowed through her blood and it lay in her heart.
> The stream meandered through hedgerowed meadows;
> The maid went to live in Witches' Hollow.

The sun basked greenly on weeping willows;
The trees framed the entrance to Witches' Hollow.
A rotund shape flitted gently through the gloom;
The third witch arrived in the valley by her broom.
She held no illusions; her face shone not fair;
She trod the way of the sisters from the Isle of the Mare.
A quiet wisdom and a listening ear,
A countenance designed with no oddities to fear:
This she was, and yet with the power that she held,
Many a foul creature or foeman had been felled.
> The sun, in the background, lit up the meadows;
> The light found its way into Witches' Hollow.

The crone, by the broom-flowers white and yellow,
Awaited the visitors to Witches' Hollow.
The wood was gathered and the fire was lit,
And all upon the mossy rocks the trio did sit:
The very first coven on our land's ancient ground,
For in need were the peasants and farmers all around;
With the sharp minds and kindness shown by sisters of
   the Mare,
Plans were designed, and pupils trained there,
Their spells and potions to be utilized for good,
In that mystical hollow 'twixt the hills and the woods.
    The work they had wrought there none could
   follow:
    The three began the magic of Witches' Hollow.

The wind blew warm from the mountain's shadow;
The good village folk came to Witches' Hollow.
Grandmothers, goodmen, and little children all
Bore gifts, and all were cheerful, however large or small.
The old witches smiled as they gave out their lore;
There was rowan and bayleaf from ceiling to floor;

The world and the Hollow were friendly neighbours
    then;
Sisters and brothers were witches and men;
The message was spread from the Isle of the Mare:
That magic existed to make the world fair;
        The path through the woods lay for all to follow;
        The path led down into Witches' Hollow.

The trees of the wood cast their dark green shadows;
The noon becomes old in Witches' Hollow.
A priestly delegate arrives in the town,
A black-cowled man come straight from the Crown.
In the Hollow, a raven alights upon a chair:
Caws at the shrine for the sisters of the Mare.
A new religion rises, demanding blood;
The path through the woods is blackening with mud.
The evening comes faster; the day is growing old;
The visitors are fewer, their gazes wide and cold.
        The wind moans eerily about the windows;
        Lonely and lonelier is Witches' Hollow.

The sun sets on lilies drifting in the shallows;
The night descends upon Witches' Hollow.
Burning torches pierce the silken night;
The villagers are ready, to hunt and to fight!
The magic ones look, and hide in the woods;
Some leave the Hollow, disguised by their hoods;
The broom and the ferns are torn asunder,
Screams arise with the night of the hunter!
All pleas to the sisters of the Isle of the Mare,
From the wise, from the learning, are lost in the air!

    The night moves and keens with an untold sorrow,

    But nothing moves or breathes in Witches' Hollow.

XXVI

NIGHT-TIME

It's night-time now, and I go to bed, but not to fall asleep;
Instead, I dream of the summertime and I feel like a wandering sheep:
No-one knows the cry of a lamb that, godless, alone does roam,
And no-one hears the beat of a heart that knows no truth in its home;
It's night-time now, and wet with tears is the book of the search for truth;
Can *you* be so cruel? oh, they must be wrong! what is faith in this book uncouth?
They think they know you, know you so well, like a son his father knows,
But how can they find all your truth divine in a book and a world full of woes?
I dreamt of the snow, and then you were there, and the snow and the world were warm,

And I thought: 'No more shall I stand alone, like the
   blind sheep lost in a storm,'
Not free of doubt, but free from *them*! and I thanked
   you with words untold;
Behold, I realise what gifts you gave, and the bright
   future my life holds—
What future, though? have I got it yet? I sit up and
   prepare to go,
I stand at the door, and I make to knock, but the hand is
   tired and slow!
I grow so weary of hypocrites, of them that mock our
   ways;
They have drained your power, and tarnished your
   blood, and sent us alone through the days—
I have doubted, yes, with convenient lies; but your
   proofs are stronger than mine;
So beautiful—so indescribable—a love we can never
   define;
What are you—and where—and how—and why? I fear
   we shall never know,
But the dream is past—my life is here; and I knock at
   the door and I go.

XXVII

ANOTHER BRICK IN THE WALL

In this dreary classroom:
shades of blue and white and grey,
sitting amongst the same old books,
repeating the same old days.
I wish I were scaling the mountain cold,
the wind whipping this grey-brown hair;
mist and dew and frost underfoot—
but in this poor grey place I hold no care…
I wish I were pretty; I wish I were petite,
I wish my locks were blond rather than brown—
but in this simple navy uniform
all shred of inspiration is broken down.
I return myself to the crowd in this chamber,
disciple of boredom and banality drear,
like everyone, here—the roar of Education
encroaching the boundaries within our ears!

XXVIII

ON THE DISCOVERY OF WINTER

What happened to the Sun?
  Our faces miss his kiss that lights the air;
  Upwards we glance—his golden cloak's not there!
Can he not chase the clouds away
  With lashings of his belligerent stare?

What happened to the Sun?
  Always he let us know when it was day;
  He'd stand outside and shine in our caveways;
He'd make the girls and women smile
  And say to him, 'Sun, what a lovely day!'

What happened to the Sun?
  Without a torch on his way, is he lost?
  Did he find beds of snow and fog and frost
On his long journey through the sky?
  What waylaid him, and what could be the cost?

What happened to the Sun?
  Has he grown tired of making joyful light?
  Does he long for the cool stillness of night?
He cannot have forsaken us;
  O Sun, return, and glint in our sight!

XXIX

SLEEP

So when she sleeps, to slumber deep,
  Her eyelids dank and dark with tears,
Don't wake her! in her dream she weeps,
  In lands of Fancy fights her fears.
Don't wake her! though her hands be cold,
  And chill creep o'er her nose and ears,

And lips sigh fantasies untold;
    Don't wake her! 'tis not for you to hear!
And as she lies, don't touch her hair,
    Or tempt your lips to kiss her face;
Don't covet what her body wears;
    If you'd respect her, grant her space:
Casting eyes o'er forbidden ground
    And lusting that you cannot see,
Is that the way she'd want you 'round—
    To leer like tattooed men at sea?
Keep your distance—respect her dreams!
    Let restful sleep her comfort be;
Wait you, until she wakeful seems;
    Don't overwhelm her—let her see
The best, and, yea, the worst of you;
    So court her in true honesty,
And one day, yea, she may be true
    To you who touched her not in sleep!

XXX

THE MINOR GODS

Chance with his bloodshot eyes and jester's hat;
Death with her blood-stained robe and icy axe;
Time with eyes like clocks and dress like mirror;
War with the helm smitten through by the sabre;
Destiny cloaked with her hair in braids;
Fear that is crawling with sickness in the shade;
Hope with hair golden, diamond in her eyes;
History who maps the playground of Time;
Joy who has hair as orange as a carrot;
Freedom with flags who walks around naked!

XXXI

LIMITLESS

Limitless are my boundaries
    And limitless is my pain;
He always finds his way around me
    Again and again and again;
Limitless is his duplicity
    And limitless are his lies;
Sometimes I try to find the life for me,
    Until I see myself in his eyes
        And I stop trying.

XXXII

STARS

Six months ago, then he walked away,
    And the silence in my life became stunning.
The telly was on, and I heard the news:

That the cosmic comet was coming.
It was six months ago when he walked away,
   Like a thief, in the night with his cunning.

The comet has passed, with a flaring light,
   Like a signal fire in the sky;
I look up at the night, at the Southern Cross,
   And a little tear drops from my eye;
The comet has passed, like a fallen seraph,
   And still in my doorway sit I.

And I wonder, as I look up at the Cross,
   Does a humanoid with eyes like mine,
A girl like me, perhaps, with a lovely face
   From which gifts of the Graces do shine;
Does she look up at me, and wonder like I,
   Is there a humanoid with graces like mine?

For so far here on Earth, no heart have I found
   I could eternally call all my own,
And I think I may be doomed to bear my old age
   As a spinster, abandoned and alone—

But ye stars! do you speak? is there a heart for
    me,
    Is there, somewhere, an answer to my moan?

Perhaps, in the gaseous, poisonous blanket
    Of Venus, there lives a lonely man
In a little community of Earth's runaways,
    Whom the stars every evening does scan;
Perhaps, on his gaseous, poisonous planet,
    For my heart, there's a way and a plan!

Perhaps there is war between the Centauri stars,
    And a dark-eyed military king
Prepares to attack the reprehensible foe,
    Then returns, to continue ruling
With no queen by his side, and wages his war
    Against corrupted and evil things!

Perhaps, in a city on the belt of Orion,
    Great scientists watch as they please,
With their knowledge so ancient, our lives here
    on Earth,

And, maybe, an astronomer sees,
There on his planet on the belt of Orion,
With tenderness, my heart on its knees.

Perhaps, far beyond Andromeda, the folk
Are primitive and dwelling in woods,
And perhaps by his fire a savage lone-wolf,
A man with no woman or goods,
Does sit by his fire, oh! light-years away,
And sigh, for his lonlisome moods!

Perhaps, in the holes and the spaces between,
A little ship moves on its way,
With one astronaut, who travels all alone
Because nobody bids him to stay;
A single spaceman on a one-man cruise,
In the dark, lonely spaces far away.

Or perhaps there is simply no comfort, no heart
In all of the wide Galaxy
That was made just for mine, and withers apart
Without contact or comfort from me!

Oh, surely there must be somebody's heart
   In all of the wide Galaxy!

If only someone in this world would hear
   The cry from my unheeded soul,
And find me, when both of us no more could bear
   To be far from our mutual goal—
Oh, that one in the world I would cherish and keep
   'Til the stars themselves burned out, burned to coal!

XXXIII

SPRINGTIME

Skippering, rollicking, gracefully frolicking
   Down the hills and into the meads;
Jumping, landing, gently meandering
   Through the valley and down to the feed.

Not biting—nibbling; arguing, quibbling
    Over the feed inside the trough;
Dancing and jittering, jigging and flittering—
    Hope they'll stop before they're too rough!
Then with a bicker, a fast faery flicker,
    Down the path with tossing of head;
Skippering, rollicking, gracefully frolicking—
    Let them be free without any dread!

XXXIV

THE WIZARD

He sits atop his empty tower,
    Overlooking the river Wrede;
Sees the garden with dew-drops ashower,
Roses with petals all haughty and white,
The walls laid in with copper and silver,
The luckless room that he lives in,
This year's daisies, and sorcery-flowers,

    And the forest where magic ever lies and
breeds.

This forest—Cirthclaeon—grows tall and wild,
    And no brave hero dares to enter there,
So by the maze of trees he is exiled—
Lonely, forever!—his heart does cry out;
Lonely, forever!—from the four walls he riles,
Lonely, and trapped, in his own slow decay!
But he remembers, once! a fairy-child
    With the fairest of minds, and small hands,
and wild hair!

So he remembers how (was it so long ago?
    It could be yesterday!) a seeming young baby
Stepped out of the woods and halted the flow
Of the river Wrede, which turned to ice,
By merely touching her littlest toe
On the crest of the seething waves.
She hesitated first, then, with a slow
    Sad smile to the woods, she crossed the river
clearly!

As she went, she changed, grew up, grew older,
    From baby, to toddler, then grew to maiden;
Her step grew surer, her gaze grew bolder,
And, watching now, he scarce could tear his eyes
From the lovely woman, who standing on the border
Of the stream, did smile her slow, sad, sweet smile
And bid the waves fall back into order.
    She stood—he stared—she looked up—their eyes met, then!

He ran out of his tower—he ran down the stair,
    Snatching the first of his robes that came by chance;
As he opened the doors, she was standing there,
In all her beauty, unclothed and unjewelled,
Eyes of blue ice, and long, long hair,
Which curled and waved and moved as though alive;
Never had he seen one so wild and so fair!

He held out the robe—she smiled as though entranced!

He showed her the castle—he took her all over,
    And told her about all his hopes and creations,
Offered to teach her sorcery that would help her;
Asked her of her name—she replied: 'Cirnay.'
She asked him of his work, the noble magicker;
She told him she had come with powers beyond the woods
To cure his loneliness and calm his heart's fear;
    'But never!' he cried, 'have I felt such fair sensations!

'So long have I lived in this tower in the woods,
    So long have I dreamt that I were not alone,
Now you are here—and floods, the sweetest floods
Of love, does my heart bestow upon you, maiden!'
But he did not know, as he never could,
Of an evil watching, waiting to strike:
Liltcapon the Black, prince of dark and blood,
    Who'd known fair Cirnay as some other one!

She had been born a changeling fair
    To a common kitchen servant:
And even when young, her untamed hair
Had been cause for lordly concern.
The wicked prince got to know her, watched her with care;
Made plans to lure her to his bed:
So entranced was he by her fire and dare,
    That he wanted her, though just a lowly servant!

But Cirnay heard of his foul plan, and so she ran away,
    And found the forest Cirthclaeon,
An ancient place where magic still held sway;
There she dwelt, and watched the magician
In his dreary dwelling, alone day after day;
So she used the power to her bequeathed,
And some which the Forest gave away,
    To cross the magic river, and live to love on!

Cirnay, she thought, had found her true love:
    For weeks they were merry together,
And as one of the fairy-folk it did behove,
She gave her wizard nought but merriness:
They sang, they laughed, they danced, they loved;
Happy, fulfilled, he was, she was;
They swore by powers below and above
    That always Love would bind them together!

But, after weeks had gone by, there came a night
    Cirnay did feel cold on her face:
She got out of bed; she made a small light,
Stared out of the window, where darkness was,
Seeing nothing, went back; pulled the sheets tight,
'Til, too late, she realised—the dark was too dense,
The evening stars should've been shining bright—
    She got up, she gripped her fighting mace!

Too late! for Liltcapon was in the room!
    Reared himself up to demon height;
His impenetrable black bulk loomed
And he roared with rage and evil!

The wizard woke—too late, his doom
Was sealed in the eyes of Liltcapon:
Strive he did to escape his tomb—
    Then cried Cirnay, 'The light! the light!'

She called up a wall of fairy light;
    The creature by this was blinded,
Shrieked in a breath of vengeance and spite,
And lashed his tentacles out—
The wizard called up an abyss of light,
Into which Liltcapon dropped,
Black, vicious creature of hatred and blight—
    But wait! Cirnay's by his tentacle binded!

And as the wizard caught the hand of his beloved
    The abyss was slowly shutting,
And as all the colours shifted and moved
A chill shot through Cirnay,
For as the spiked tentacle had forcibly moved
Its poison had punctured her skin;
She fell down limp and did not move;
    The wizard fell by her, bitterly weeping!

She was dead—no magic could change that state,
    Though he tried, and all in vain;
Though he screamed his defiance at cruelty of Fate,
She cold and limp, unresponsive, did stay!
He dug a grave by the pond where she'd sat,
And wept on the cold memorial-stone,
And wailed his sorrow, too late, too late,
    Though thanked the gods, that she'd had little pain!

And now his eyes do stray,
    Like traitors, to the little pond,
And he sits like a stone, this sunny day,
Alone in his tower so cold.
The flowers bloom the year away;
It's never winter here,
But read the hopeless words his soul does pray:
    'Come back! my heart, so fond!

'Without you, my life is empty;
    Without you, the flowers are grey;
Without you, the birdies' sweet melody
Is monotonous, flat, and drear!
I stare at the floating water-lilies,
Seeing you on the stream-bank,
A tender child, stepping over to me;
    Come back! come back, my heart, my day!
    Cirnay! Cirnay! my soul weeps and prays!'

XXXV

THE SPELL

This is the road to Fist,
  Wreathed with a cloak of mist,
And wet in the rain is the oncoming train,
  But, slowly, they persist.
  A path the road does cross;
  Leads to a cave of moss;
Its grey-blackened stones are strewn with bones,

And shadows dance all across.
A deathly fire blights
The straggling morning light,
And a pot bubbles green with a mixture unclean
   And foul to anyone's sight.
   She tends the pot and fire,
   Black hair like metal biers,
And her eyes gleaming red in the gaze so dread
   Of the awful, arcane pyre.
   Anon she hums a chant,
   As she adds the tiger ants,
And the lacewing flies with their myriad eyes;
   Anon she hums a chant:

'His hair as black as death,
   Clean mornings on his breath,
Eyes that are green as you've never never seen
   Like the moss that grows on the heath.
   Swift with spear and bow,
   A deep voice gentle and low,

And whistle strong, yet like the thrushes' song
  Beneath his sad-looking brow.
  The voice of a wildman hoarse,
  Yet gallant for better or worse;
His torso is strong and his strides are long,
  A master to hawk and horse;
  Respect his face commands;
  No fear before him stands;
His chin and lips are as stubborn as the tips
  Of spears in soldiers' hands.
  Both friends and strangers see
  That he is the knight for me,
And our castle stands in the fertile lands
  'Twixt the inlands and the sea.
  Our children are charming and gay;
  They light the rooms with their play;
Boys there are four, and the girls, twice more;
  'Tis beautiful to see them pray!

'This life I shall call to me,
  And for ever it shall be
That a courageous knight lives in palace white

Along with his fair lady.
O spirits of the hills!
Bind him by your wills,
And let the knight come to my arms, his home,
Where he'll bide 'til time lies still.
O spirits of the moor!
Change as it was before!
With my arcane arts and my lonely heart
I beg you, forevermore!
By fairy hands and wings,
The craft of the Mage it brings
All the hopes of the years; though I have shed tears
I can call to me—anything!
Lonely, I no more!
Longing, I no more!
My own destiny does fall now to me,
With my magic from the core!
O let the wild winds blow,
Let the sea come and go,
Let Change rear his head o'er the worldly dead
And let the change come now!'

The pot hisses and steams;
  From its grooves there drip three streams,
And they sneak in the cracks, and flow to the
    track
  From whence the raindrops gleam.
  The road to Fist is long,
  But the magic streams are strong,
And they reach the train in the sullen rain
  As they glisten all along!

XXXVI

BLACK RIBBON

In the abyss so far from here,
  Black ribbon 'round us,
No blissful, peaceful sleep,
  No light to bind 'round us.

Waiting in the darkness,
    No knowledge to coin us,
Waiting for some other
    Unfortunate to join us.

Carrion crows circle
    In the air above us,
Picking at our bodies
    Like denizens that love us.

Curst be the mighty hand
    That into life cast us
And drove us, ever forward,
    Into the blackness past us!

The abyss so far from here,
    Where our sin devours us,
Here we wait.—waiting,
    With black ribbon 'round us.

XXXVII

GUNS

Derelict and dusty is the courtyard where we live,
But underneath these rusted roofs there is so much to give;
They meet at night, when no-one sees, and plot their deadly plans;
They harry us to take up guns, and spare not a single man;

A sleepy silence hushes over the creaking joists and blocks,
We doze beneath the iron roof, secure behind our locks;
Of a sudden there comes an engine's roar, and the yells of infantry;
My sisters and I all huddle close, and Mama, she clings to me—

They have gutted the rebels' meeting-house, and shot them one by one;

They have ransacked our place, and gone through our
    homes, and threatened the lives of our sons;
A blood-red sun comes up in the east, for the dawn is
    stained with blood;
The time for shouting is long past gone: they cannot
    contain this flood;

With eyes averted, faces hid, we sidle about our ways;
And they think they have won, and go back home,
    leaving the dead where they lay;
And new rebels rise in our tired streets, even more
    blood-starved than the last,
And they condemn us all as cowards' sons, who will not
    partake in the blast;

And the gun-metal feels so cold and dead underneath
    my living skin;
Dead, we all—yes, they do not care—we have borne so
    much hatred and sin;
Mama patted me on the back and told me that no-one
    was going to die,

But when I left her alone, and sat at the door like a child, I could hear her cry.

Saturday morning—the Sun rises all in a glow of red:
The Sun has a coronet of blood upon his gentle head;
Passed from child to parent are the roaring, blazing guns;
The township takes her liberty back, and pays with the lives of her sons;

Saturday night—my eyes are closed in a hellish haze of red;
My sisters die with collars of blood around their beautiful heads;
Passed from child to parent are the roaring, blazing guns—
Freedom is dead—and so am I—you have paid with the lives of your sons.

XXXVIII

HITMAN

I lied.
I said it didn't matter.
That's the worst lie that I've ever told,
because I broke the heart that was made of gold.
Now you're a lovesick man on a mission.
Is there a word for all of this pain?
I'm trembling and I'm shaking, and I'm moving too slow;
now you're a hitman, a hitman, what do you know?
I lost my body and my brain, and now it's getting too much;

can you save me, can you love me, with a single magic touch?
Just know I'm free—
I don't know who I am, but I'm me,
and I'll never admit I lied.

I hurt you.
I told you I didn't love you.
It's a nightmare of mine
I've been having for some time.
Now you're a lovesick man on a mission.
I try to deny the way I felt when you held me
so tenderly that I thought the world was all right again.
But the world is still sick, and I'm coughing and I'm dying;
I'm a patient, I'm an invalid, I'm dying just for you,
but I can feel you: if you touch me, it could be magic once again.
Just know I'm free—
I don't know who the hell I am, but I'm me,
and I'll never know how the hell you thought you could love me.

XXXIX

MARY JANE

How swiftly the years have raced!
   Now she stands in another place,
And the hardness and cruelty of all the years
   Are etched in the lines of her face.

Oh Love! if only there were
   Another chance to see or to hear
Her face—or her song, my penance be done
   And dried up my very last tear.

But she stands in another place,
   And another beholds her face,
And he owns and controls all her memories,
   So of me she recalls no trace.

XL

MIA

Twenty-five years ago today,
   I heard and saw you say, 'I do.'
Your small dark hands lifted to pray;
   I whispered, 'Mia, I do too.'

From two firm streets of black and white
   We started out, and met midway;
Cared not if Love was wrong or right,
   But took his path—the trail of grey.

In all the years that since are past,
   They said we'd never make it here,
But here we are—and at long last,
   Love's triumphed over hate and fear.

Our oldest girl's a-married now,
   And still I hear you say, 'I do';
I'll stick to honour and my vow;
   I'll shout now: Mia, I do too!

XLI

THE STUDENT'S PLEA TO MINERVA

Minerva, Minerva, what's happened to me?
Spaced out on question
Number five point three,
Oh dearie me, dearie me, what have I done?
My pen out of ink
And my time overrun!
Watch me now, watch as I fiddle and fret;
Chew at my pencil,
How could I forget?
Headmaster, Mistress, believe me—it's true:
It's not that I'm slacking,
There's just so much to do!
Minerva, Minerva, you must hear my plea,
All that I need
Is my anatomy!

XLII

THE FANTASY

One night I was sitting in my study full of books
   — I was savouring them one by one:
All those dreams, those wild stories, all at my command
   To be studied, understood, and won—
When suddenly a darkness fell upon the room
   As the candles snuffed themselves out,
And a wind rose, to blow 'round the things on my desk
   And to howl both within and without:
It could have raised the dead from their mystic sleep,
   And a beam of light shone on the floor;
I stood nearer, entranced, to the disembodied light,
   And my soul felt as though it could soar,
For out of the beam stepped a tall fair Elf,
   With a quiver and bow in his hands,
And bound in his hair was a clear stone of blue

That shone with the light of far lands.
And then there sounded hoofbeats, and into the room
  A magnificent stallion rode,
A steed fit for kings, and on his shoulders white
  He bore the proudest and noblest of loads:
A warrior of Men, with a black-bright sword,
  A weapon stained with goblins' blood,
Weary with travel, and dusty with the road,
  The hooves of his mount caked in mud.
As I wondered at the pair, then more swiftly came:
  A family of doughty Dwarfs,
Bearded and chainmailed, from granther to wife,
  Bearing axes clean enough to eat off.
A pale silhouette in the beam announced the next:
  A Lady robed all in white;
Raven was her hair, and noble her brow,
  And in her hands, a stone of light.
Then a sulphurous flame rose up and licked the roof,
  And a creature arose from the smoke:
Reptilian, scaled, and glowing like an ember,

A Dragon to endure no yoke:
For in his fiery eyes a millennium of lore
   Looked down upon me, a mere girl,
And such power was contained in those wings and those jaws
   That to feel it made my very hair curl.
Though they filled my little room quite up to the roof
   This was never the end of the troupe:
I gazed upon the shadows that were moving in the beam
   And my stomach gave a sickening loop:
In the centre of the circle of the bright beam of light
   Came a black so complete and deep
That just to focus on it was a jolt to the eyes
   And quite fit to make a shaman weep.
I saw a handle of wood, and a long, shining blade,
   And a long, flowing robe with a hood;
And under this cover of ebony, a skull
   With a grin that transfixed me where I stood.

As Death stood in my study like a vision come to life,
    All I could do was gape and stare,
But even as I watched, his bones faded away
    To be covered by wrinkles and hair.
His beard it grew long, and his face became wise,
    And his scythe was replaced by a staff;
The Wizard looked upon me, and bent his lofty head,
    And laughed a great, loud, booming laugh—
With a gasp I awoke, with my cheek upon a book,
    And I shook my head sadly at myself;
I stood up from my chair, snapped the paperback closed,
    And replaced the little book on the shelf.
Then my attention was caught by some object on the mat,
    And to know what it was, I could not fail,
For never more mundane is any fantasy-thought
    Than the hair from a white horse's tail!

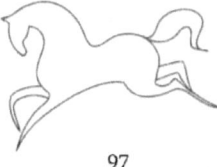

XLIII

THE HERO WITHIN

I woke up in a dream,
  Black webs all over me;
Cried out and reached for you—
  Found nothing; you're too busy.
I woke up all alone;
  I went walking in the night;
I called to you in the rain,
  I prayed to make things right;
Yes, I have loved you so,
  A love born out of sin;
O what would it take not to light the road ahead,
  For you to flee from the hero within?

In the streets of rage and shame
  You go walking, all alone;
You fear no-one and no pain;
  Where you pass, there is no more moan;

Invisibly silent, you walk;
  Where you tread, there is no more fear;
Through so many roads you go,
  But never do you set foot here;
There is silence in the palace you built;
  There is nothing but pain and fear;
No hero's footsteps falling;
  No shoulder to own my tears.
You are far from the home that you built;
  You're a legend about to begin;
O what would it take for you to turn from the streets,
  For you to flee from the hero within?

I am far from the dangers you face,
  A remnant forgotten and dead,
A memory without a name,
  Left behind as you passed on ahead.
No more do you stand by my side;
  No more are your heavy hobnailed boots
Plodding by with their mournful tread;
  The sounds that I knew are all mute.

Why harp on about your boots?
  Every morsel of you is mine;
One day—one day you may remember
  The maid whom you left far behind;
And the fiery hussy in your arms,
  The prize for the war that you fought,
And the myriad sons that she bore,
  And her lust for you—shall all count as nought;
You shall retread the derelict lanes
  That you trod on to gain your renown,
But though this maze for ever you weave,
  The storm-weathered palace of stone
That you built when your years were few,
  Will be all in your labyrinth lost,
And the lady who pined so for you
  Will be dead, and grown over with frost.
You will call out my name in the streets,
  You will scream out your prayers in the rain,
You will pass by the life you once knew,
  And, at last, you will come to know my pain.
Was it worthwhile, then, in the end,

To forsake me for glory's win?
O what can be done, for you to feel the same as I,
So you will flee from the hero within?

Remember: to me you belong;
I can call upon the oath you once made;
You were more like a hero then,
When your honour was the words that you said.
Remember: I know your every part;
I know every thought and each fear;
And I know that the chasm in your heart
Has a healing which is only found here.
Why, then, do you walk away from me?
Can the love I feel so purely be a sin?
O what would it take for you to turn back to me,
For you to flee from the hero—the coward—within?

XLIV

HOME

Through the gorgeous halls of the cheerful folk,
    Unnoticed, she does roam;
And she lingers there, resenting his watch:
    Silence, to take her home.
And she dwells on the things of her day-by-day,
    What her dreary life does own:
No laughter, no colour—and Silence, he waits:
    Waiting, to take her home;
And her home crumbles up, burns up in her mind—
    But she's not blind:
    She must go home.

Silence, he leads, and she follows the way,
    And the raindrops all come down,
Drenching, but teasing like puppies at play,
    Just as quickly grown.
In torrents they walk, but her grief she forgets;
    Tries to play with the rain;

With the beautiful drops, with the wind, in the wet,
    Laughing at all of her pain.
But Silence he stops, and she knows she must cease—
    For her, no peace—
    She leaves the rain.

The mist and fog all seem to enshroud
    This apparition, home,
Coloured with iron-grey, and black stormcloud;
    She slacks, she starts to moan.
But there's no comfort, for Silence, he waits,
    Waiting outside her home;
She knows, once inside, there is no respite
    From the grief that she knows is her own,
And only Silence keeps her company,
    All silently,
    And all alone.

She dreams on the halls of red, green and blue,
    But wakes up, all alone;
She dreams of the cold of the cleansing rain,
    But wakes up, safely enzoned.

And Silence, he watches over all her dreams
    So none can be only her own;
And in the hall of brightness, the people laugh,
    Her plight to them unknown,
Whilst she fights for her dreams—she hopes, one day,
    No longer to pray,
    But to go home.

XLV

TO A DEAD SWALLOW BY THE SIDE OF THE ROAD

Poor bird! that lies now on the tarmac,
   Lifeless, limp and growing cold;
   Your brimming eyes, that seem so old,
That must have seen so many things, gone
     black.

Poor bird! if you could tell of sights
   You saw when you were young,
   When tunefully way up high you sang
As you gazed down upon the city lights—

Poor bird! though now I pity you,
   Too many were the days
   That you flew as I came your way,
And I wished my heart could be soaring too!

Poor bird! as you flapped in the morning
   breeze,
   What secrets might there be,
   What sights saw you on the wide wide sea,
Ere you flapped your last and your breathing
   ceased?

For you saw such wonders in flight,
   Poor bird, in faraway lands,
Of the bronzed sun setting on tropical strands,
And the statues of yore, that impressively
   stand,
And the hallowed dawn held in His ancient
   hands;
   Poor bird, indeed! in your flights,
You have seen so much more than I!
And while my life peters out, with a slow-
   moving blight,
The beauties you've beheld still shine from
   your eye!

XLVI

POLYHYMNIA

These footways once by thee were trod,
   In years too old to say,
When in these forests heathen gods
   Controlled the course of day.
And in these clearings, fires were lit
   And flutes played all the night;
They danced, then, danced; they could not sit;
   So gave the gods their right—

Fauns musical, and centaurs tall
   Honoured thy name in song;
At winter's end, with summer's fall
   They celebrated long;
Groves haunted with piper's music,
   Dales of daffodils,
Tall oaken-trees, and rushes thick
   Were there to ode at will—

Fair Nature gave the gift to hear,
    And from thy lips was cried
The first great song—those verses dear
    Have ne'er yielded or died.
The leaping flames reflect the notes
    So longing and so pure;
'Twas caught by Man, and from his throat
    Thy songs they loved to hear!

The fire is dead, and ash remains;
    From such malnourishment
My body barely life retains,
    And all that I am sent
Are scraps and leavings, such as would
    Make Charon's soul decay;
But none remember, none that could,
    And so things fade away—

Thy followers, they spanned the seas,
    Too many for to count;
Thou filled'st the hopes and hearts of these,
    And wealthy was the bount'!

On beaches were thy footprints seen,
    On stormy cliffs thy dance;
In Neptune's spray, in tempests keen,
    Thy glorious shining glance—

To highest peaks, to swirling deeps,
    Were brought thy graces fair;
Thou took'st a tear from him who weeps,
    From her that laughs, a hair;
The dark hair drifted free from fear,
    And itched beneath the skin,
So brought forth words, which by the tear
    Were cleansed, and shone within—

They built for thee a tower strong
    In trees of tropic lands;
They brought thee gifts of mystic songs
    From their own, gentle hands;
Thou gav'st them milk and luscious fruit
    So they might wake and sing,
And in their love, ne'er were they mute,
    But offered everything—

Immortal poets! sing for me,
    So I may travel far,
To be as you, so wild and free,
    Beneath the dancing stars;
Let me believe, for once! that you
    Have come to victory,
As you cross countries fair and new
    And far beyond the sea—

Lo! beauty lives within the isle;
    Is uttered in a song;
And this sweet sound doth sail a mile
    As nymphs all hum along;
In wonder, pirates, soldiers, serfs
    Do hear the haunting notes;
For once the Sirens feel no mirth
    For songs from different throats—

Alas! alas! I cannot hear
    The fleeting Muse's joy;
I clutch at tendrils; burning tears

    Taunt my eyes with annoy!
Where art thou now? not here, not here!
    These ling'ring dated lines
Are all that 'mains of thee, I fear,
    And only I be thine!

I see the sunset, feel the rain;
    I stand upon thy grave;
Thou lost them all, with mother's pain,
    And no more gifts thou gave'st,
For none are worthy—none do dwell
    In romance and with rhyme;
Thy stories died with none to tell,
    And sadly now, thou yield'st to Time.

XLVII

THE CRACKED MIRROR

There's a cracked, cracked mirror in the
  bathroom, bathroom,
    A split like the Grand Canyon;
And wherever I go, they leer and they jeer
    As I struggle to sing my song—
I stared at myself: my eyes, my eyes
    Were detached from my crooked nose;
Oh why should I care, should I blink, should I
  cry;
    Can my bloom be so far from the rose?
Look at me, selfish mirror: tell me true, tell
  me true,
    Do you twist my reflection to rights?
What I see, and you see, is it not the same?
    I search myself beneath the spotlights,
But all that I find is all that I found
    In the years and the times long before;
So weary am I, so far from the truth;

    So removed from this world, and more—
In the cracked, cracked mirror on the
    bathroom wall
        I scream at myself in despair,
But what has passed here can only be read
    By one who knows the currents of the
    air.

XLVIII

IT FEELS LIKE FREEDOM

Alone, alone, all, all alone;
It feels like freedom, all alone.
I wish that I were going home,
Where it feels like freedom, all alone.

A lover's arms, a darkened room,
Some DVDs to pass the night;
Time comes, and leaves again so soon,
Leaves memories in her precious flights.

I wish that I were going home;
Come set me on that motorbike,
And send me down the lanes I've known,
Where beggars shout and troopers hike.
The bus glides down the stony roads,
Illumined by the city lights;
In every street, there beats a code
Made by the city for her rights.
I search not for the lofty beat
Made by the stately city halls;
I need the code that earths my feet
And draws my nature whole and all:
It beats, 'Here from these humble streets
A lonely pilgrim wandered far,
To carry proof of our streets
Unto lands unfamiliar.
Where she bides now, is not her home';
I wish that I were all alone;
Not hard as rock, not cold as stone,
But filled with freedom, going home.
A demon whispers in my ear:
'So wrong,' he murmurs, 'everyone;

Why should you have to fret and fear?
Go follow freedom, in the sun.'
I wish I were a stronger being,
Who waltzed along without a doubt,
And waved my banner red and green,
And made me heard with every shout.
I wish that I were walking home,
The rotting city in my face,
On blighted streets, to walk alone,
And to feel free with every pace.
I wish my eyes were bright again,
As they will be when doubt has gone,
So far removed from all this pain,
And filled with freedom, going home.
I'll work this week, for every home;
I'll bear with them to be alone;
When Sunday comes, I'll be in town,
Where it feels like freedom, going home.

XLIX

AIMLESSLY LOOKING FOR MY LOVE

    It's a very pretty morning;
The bite and leaves of Fall are in the air.
    And, as usual, without warning,
Beyond my bed—my doorway—he was there.
    No rest for me today, it seems,
For all my aims are Alpine and above:
    With nought but morn and midnight dreams,
I'm wandering aimlessly, looking for my Love.

    His figure was before my sight;
I felt him, heard him, smelled his freckled skin,
    Then he was gone, like endless flight
Of autumn leaves heavenward fluttering.
    I sought him in the city streets,
In human haunts both under and above,
    But swift, invisible his feet,
So I wander aimlessly, looking for my Love.

The thought of him burns vividly
Above and beyond all worldly aches or cares,
    And I seek him in honesty
To lay my soul upon his altar, bare.
    He does not dwell with other men
Where laughing, talking everywhere they move,
    But far from knowledge is his den,
So far from me, aimlessly looking for my Love.

    What shall I do, if finally
I reach into the mists and feel his hand;
    If, suddenly, he'd follow me,
Enchanted, loyal, all over the land?
    Shall I place chains upon his limbs
So never from my side he'll dare to move?
    Or would I, bravely, release him
Just to wander aimlessly, looking for his Love?

    If a very pretty morning
Comes across his way and stirs his wayward hair,
    Will he give me any warning,
And when it ends, at dusk, will he be there?

I never shall have rest, it seems,
For all my aims are Alpine and above;
   I'll have to work to make my dreams:
To not wander aimlessly, looking for my Love.

L

TO ANY UNIVERSITY, ANYWHERE ON EARTH

In Deo Sapentiae Lux

All day I walk, but now and then
   Up to your sea-blue skies I look,
And riches of ten million men
   Are poorer than your trove of books—

All day I work, but when the leaves
   Come dancing through the dusty sky,
And bounce and blow down iron greaves,
   I look again, and I know why.

All day in dark, but now the Sun
   Does shine upon my humble face;
I catch a leaf, wish for the one
   Who holds me in this blessed place;

All day I talk, but silence now;
   Remember what you are to me:
A sacred promise; I know how
   And why I'm here, for certainty;

One prayer for Him who yonder sees
   The light of our human lore,
And, knowing all we know is His,
   Smiles back at us—and holds the door.

LI

TIMELESS

I tried to write a poem of you,
   The way you make me feel—
I tried and toiled—then gave up,
   And it's so typical!
Your words outsmart me every day;
   When I'm eight, you're a nine;
I'm here listening to love songs
    'Cause I never get the time.

How can you be so sure and calm?
   I watch you every day:
The ways you walk, the shirts you wear,
   And constantly I pray:
Please don't ignore my aching heart:
   Be mine, be mine, be mine;
I'll just listen to these love songs
    'Cause I never have the time.

How boundlessly I'd follow you
   If you belonged to me,
And answered to my daily call;
   But—that can never be:
For you, my friend, belong to you,
   And I am only mine;
And you just don't hear my love song
    'Cause you never have the time.

Oh, where to finish, break this off?
   I cannot disengage
My mind from you; try as I might,
   An hour becomes an age;
To watch you and not comprehend—
   It feels like it's a crime;
I would go on, and never end,
    But just don't have the time.

LII

THE NAMING OF STEPHEN RAE

Why is the face you show the world that horrid
 haughty front?
How do you see what others can't, but blind to
 what I want?
I'd call you mine if ever you so much as kissed my
 cheek,
But still we're here, and we've been here for weeks
 and weeks and *weeks*!
I was so strong and driven (yes, and lonely) ere you
 came,
But now the remnant left for me is just to write
 your name,
And yes, I tried so very hard to name you for my
 verse,
But, Stephen Rae, no other name did fit you like
 your first:
My first attempt was *Asterix*, but he's gone long
 ago:

A burnt-out star, and left me with a heart of ice and snow;
Copernicus and *Galilei* were far too proud and old
For your messy hair and eyes in which lie riddles yet untold;
I then wanted to name you for some mineral or stone;
Diopside, Garnet, Amethyst, but couldn't find your own;
For, Stephen Rae, you're all to me; I cannot isolate
One single face, and name it from the whole conglomerate;
The cruellest trick up Venus' sleeve is illustrated here:
To strike a girl all through the heart and relish in her tears;
For as it is, I cannot fight as men do for their love—
That does not calm the burning ache, the daydreaming remove!
So bittersweet the feeling is, I cannot help but cry;
To hold it in when I'm with you!—oh, surely I shall die!

But would you leave me thus, and turn all you've done into wrong?
I'd like to dream my dream of you, but shall I sleep too long?
You did not sweep me off my feet with words, or wit, or rede,
But merest dreams—my fantasies—outweigh your worldly deeds;
When our hands lie side by side, the tremors fill my skin;
My breathing stops, my heart foxtrots, my soul grows warm within;
I name you matchless, name you mine; if only I knew how,
I'd be the first and last woman you'd ever want to know;
I cannot call you any other than your given name;
My all for you, my Stephen Rae—'twas peaceful 'til you came.

LIII

THE CURSE OF LARA TWILIGHT

The Whitebirch woods were aeons old;
The trees' carpet was green and gold,
And here, for years and years untold,
   Lived Lara Twilight's people.
A race with long-lived beauty blest,
They built their homes in trees, like nests;
Defended all, from east to west,
   From evil beasts and peoples.

A merry dark-haired, blue-eyed maid,
From morn to evening, Lara played,
In innocence and unafraid,
   In woods she always knew.
In youth she never knew what ailed
The adults, but she could not fail
To hear of war when it prevailed
   In woods that Lara knew.

Of evils far from home, she heard,
The warriors fought—but no thoughts stirred
In her young mind like flapping birds,
   And free from dark she sang.
Her beauty grew with passing years,
And, like a bird that knows no fear
Serenely soars the atmosphere,
   Still free from dark she sang.

And gallant youths from miles around
Came to determine by the mound
If rumours of her looks were sound,
   And stood by her astounded.
For all agreed, that such a face
Was made for love and close embrace,
And they would never leave that place,
   But stood by her astounded.

A warrior walking in the woods
Walked past the place where Lara stood;
Did not stop—but she wished he would,
   For Love had come to claim her.

The stately soldier, with his sword,
Walked past her and said not a word,
But in his mind his spirit soared,
   For Love had come to claim him.

They pledged their love in the high place
Where she would sit, and hide her face,
Resplendent in her frock of lace,
   And wait for one to love her.
The vows they made there bound their souls;
Two pieces of the same were whole;
United in one noble goal,
   She had found one to love her.

From gruesome fights which ended life,
From scenes of death and bloody strife,
The soldier returned to his wife,
   The lovely Lara Twilight.
She heard from him, marauder bands
Were fleeing, and leaving miles of land
For Lara's people to expand,
   The caresome Lara Twilight.

She bade him beat the enemy,
To show this evil no mercy,
For all his marks of victory
    Were hers to honour him with.
For clearly they were all to blame,
The enemy—and scourging flame
Would heal the world and earn him fame,
    That she could honour him with.

She sat before their woodland home,
Singing a low, enchanting tone,
When through the woods, confused, alone,
    A ragged maiden stumbled.
Her dress was torn from front to rear,
Her face was streaked with ash and tears;
She trembled and cried out with fear
    As on her feet she stumbled.

The lovely Lara Twilight cried,
And bade the poor girl come inside,
Before she tumbled down and died,

   Collapsed with fits of sobbing.
She sat in Lara's home, and spoke
Of dreadful armies; burning, smoke—
Until from weariness she broke
    Into a fit of sobbing.

The soldier arrived home that night
To find all lanterns burning bright
'Round one poor wretch in dreadful plight
    Being tended by his Lara.
But as he entered through the door,
She did not lie there anymore;
She screamed and kicked, fell to the floor
    Struggling against his Lara.

She screamed: 'His army—he's the one
Who burned my town—from whom I run—
They chased us with their swords for fun
    And slaughtered our children!
They've swept a bloody arc 'cross land
In fierce, bloodthirsty, shrieking bands—
So many have died by their hands

>Along with our children!'

She looked at him with blazing eyes;
Though Lara Twilight was not wise,
She saw now clearly all the lies
>That she had been believing.
In his hard face she read the truth;
His silent frown was all the proof;
She drew his sword, the blade uncouth,
>And broke her heart believing.

Throughout the woods the silence hung,
'Til Lara Twilight fell, and wrung
Her hands—then through the night it rang,
>The curse of Lara Twilight.
She cursed the man who'd brought her love;
She cursed the people she once loved;
She cursed the trees that stretched above
>The corpse of Lara Twilight.

The spring-green boughs began to rot;
Her people's homes collapsed in rot;

Their cries her vengeance heeded not,
   But destroyed Lara's people.
And each one dead was not released,
But trapped in spirit, not to peace
But to a torment ne'er to cease
   For Lara's cursèd people.

The wretched maiden ran from there,
From foul black smoke that burned the air,
From hideous beasts with hungry stares
   And stinking, sloughing corpses.
Where Lara lay, the grass was dead;
No life in Whitebirch more; instead
The slimy things that prowled her bed
   Were decomposing corpses.

There still she lies; her corpse is fair,
But in her sky-blue cursèd stare
She lives the truth and dreams nightmares
   In woods that once she knew.
No more the clearings where she stood
Are full of life and full of good,

But cursed the life and foul the woods
  That Lara Twilight knew.

LIV

RELATING TO LORNA DOONE

Why sit and talk? it's over now;
You know my thoughts, and God allow
You understood: for once my heart
Is given, it remains apart;
You love the maids from storybooks,
But me? how, ever, could I look
Like Lorna Doone, so beautiful
That you would love me like a fool?
You'll never see this verse I write;
You'll never learn—but if I might
Like Lorna Doone, have gentle grace
And innocence upon my face,
Would you relent to see me cry
Beneath this cloudy winter sky?

Like Lorna Doone, I long for love,
But characters that stories move
Are luckier than living men,
Especially those that grip the pen
And stain the page on which they write
With tears that fall around midnight;
You're old-fashioned, so can I ask
If you would like this worthy task:
So far removed from something new,
Like Lorna Doone, to die for you?

LV

THE BALLAD-TALE OF VAILA LANA

Come, landlord, listen; and guests, all gather round,
And let one and all feel the harp's musical sound,
For I hail from the land which is magical ground,
  From the kingdom of Vaila Lana.
There's a story we tell that entrances us still
Which occurred long ago in the woods and the hills;

Every child knows the song, and has felt its thrill
> In the kingdom of Vaila Lana.

In the springtime she sang by the brown river-bed,
Where the swans met their mates, and the trout reared their heads,
Her white feet in the water, her hair copper-red,
> In the forest of Vaila Lana.

When the weather was chill, she would dwell in the stream,
With her parents and sisters, 'neath the water's gleam,
But when the world awoke, she arose like a dream,
> The river-maid of Vaila Lana.

She sang of her home 'neath the dark river-water;
She sang of the sky, the stormy heaven-daughter;
She sang of the things that her mother taught her
> In the river of Vaila Lana.

And whilst she was singing, and sitting on the grass,
Someone chose that moment the river to pass,
And who would Fate choose, astride a fat brown ass,
> But a village-lad of Vaila Lana?

He heard the sweet notes that she sent through the
    dawn
To a tune that was softer than sunlight at morn,
And the bonny lad thought: 'Ever since I was born,
    I have dwelt here in Vaila Lana;
But never have I heard such a voice, such a song,
That could sweeten molasses, and study no wrong;
I will dismount from here, and walk the path along
    To the river of Vaila Lana.'

And when he first saw the copper-haired river-maid,
His heart filled with joy and his feet beneath him
    swayed,
As she turned then to him, on him her eyes were laid,
    That very day in Vaila Lana.
She spoke, and the music of her voice was a balm
On the noise-ravaged ears of the boy so calm,
As she quoth: 'For what reason have you ruined my
    psalm
    Of the waters of Vaila Lana?'

So he fell at her feet, and he poured out his heart:
He quoth, 'I cannot bear it; with thee I cannot part;
O say what I must do, and I shall, for thou art
    But the fairest in Vaila Lana.'
But whilst the boy was speaking, a black thunder-cloud
Did appear in the heavens, and hang like a shroud
O'er the maiden and boy, who stood with head bowed
    Before the fairest in Vaila Lana.

A white lightning-bolt split the heavens asunder;
The river-maid's heart was aroused by the thunder,
And up the stony mountain her thoughts did wander:
    To the treasure of Vaila Lana.
'There be a gem of unspeakable worth,' quoth she;
'Though kept by a dragon so big you'll seem a flea;
If your love be true, you will capture it for me,
    For the fairest in Vaila Lana.'

'Anything,' the youth cried, 'anything—and more;
Thy beauty—it is worth ten thousand books of lore;
I will climb the feared height, and brave the dragon's
    door

  For the fairest in Vaila Lana.'
As the first raindrops fell upon the rushing brook,
He was back by his mount; as the heavens shook,
The poor beast and its rider the quickest road took
  To the mountains of Vaila Lana.

Where the rocks are jagged and the cliffs are steep,
Where the mountain-devils lie snoring, asleep;
For a dragon with flame that would make a knight weep
  Climbed a boy from Vaila Lana;
He was filled with thought as he hurried up the height;
Ne'er a thought of fleeing, or a mind full of fright,
But searched for the skill to sidestep a fight
  With the dragon of Vaila Lana.

As he came to the cave, which was half up the hill,
There the dragon lay sleeping, snoring and still,
And on him the rain pouring, on him made to kill
  By the magic in Vaila Lana.
His body was the colour of bronze, and there
Was a scar by his eye like a scarlet tear;
And his scales glowed with the lightning in the air

From the storm over Vaila Lana.

With a fleet swift foot and no gestures grand,
He entered the cave and found the jewel on the sand,
And he marvelled at it, for he held in his hand
    But the treasure of Vaila Lana.
The dragon ne'er knew he was gone, or even came;
He slithered 'cross the rock in the driving rain,
And then stood at full length, to face his home again,
    And the forest of Vaila Lana.

The river-maid laughed in the mirror she had made
Out of magic, and loosened her long copper braids,
And cried, 'This is the one for whom my heart hath prayed,
    The most valiant in Vaila Lana!'
The lad stood in triumph, the gem in his fist:
'My dearest! I am coming, thro' storms and thro' mist;
Ere the morrow dawns, thy lips I will have kissed;
    But the dearest lips in Vaila Lana.'

The thunder-god looked on the lad's rightful joy,

And he laughed in the sky that he shook like a toy,
And in his wicked mind, the thought came: 'Why, this boy
    Is a hero of Vaila Lana;
If a hero he be, then lightning he can mock—'
And the god sent his bolts down the steep mountain-top—
With a heart-wrenching cry, the boy fell from the rock
    Down the cliffs of Vaila Lana.

O, terrible the cry on the river-maid's tongue!
O ended the love which had only just begun!
Yes, mourn, Vaila Lana, for the bravest of sons
    Perished on your rocks, Vaila Lana!
The river-maid rose from the waters of her home,
And ran for the strangeness of the mountain of stone;
Crouched over his body, she bore her grief alone
    For a village-lad of Vaila Lana!

And climbing the cliff, she began again to sing,
The funereal song of a maid in mourning;
Whomever's ears it reached, it would always haunt him,

All his life in Vaila Lana!
'The long years of a River-Maid's life have been spent,
And I have lost the love for which my heart was meant,
And with it the mercy which from the gods was lent,
    For my life in Vaila Lana.'

She stood on the rock from which the boy had fell;
She murmured, 'My sisters, may your lives go well';
And she leapt without fear—or so the story tells,
    From the cliffs of Vaila Lana.
And still on stormy nights, when the thunder rings loud,
And the Moon hides herself inside a cloak of cloud,
And the crops, in the rain, seem to stand with heads bowed,
    Comes a moan through Vaila Lana;
' 'Tis the maiden faery, by the dragon's cave,'
The peasants all whisper, and their faces are grave.
'For ever she is gone, but her mourning wraith
    Haunts the hills of Vaila Lana.'

LVI

RIETTA

You first bewitched me months ago,
    when icy winds did blow;
Around our cliffs the ocean moaned, our
    streets were full of snow.
I spotted you beside the street, in
    woollen dress of grey;
Your dormouse curls bounced from your
    face as winds blew hats away.
The angles of your cheekbones showed
    like rivets against your hair;
Your eyes were brown as teak but lit
    with fire in your stare;
So delicate and small you seemed, I
    almost feared for you,
But though your head scarce reached my
    chest your soul was fire too:
Those early days we fought like cats and
    dogs are wont to brawl,

But through the takes and gives of life I
    soon became your all.
Would I have loved you more if not for
    her that broke my heart?
I think so—yes, 'twas doubt and pain
    that drove our souls apart—
O fear, ye mortals, to deny the truths by
    Eros writ,
For in his rage He knows not of the
    fevers he has lit;
Rietta girl, I should have known far
    better than to play
With Love, for in his games he knows
    not what to bear away:
So you were borne away from me, as
    soon as spring began;
I would have tried to keep your heart,
    were I a nobler man,
But you were made for liberty, like oak
    leaves in a storm,
So when I woke one morning, you had
    fled with early dawn.

Long I reflected on my life, the loves that
    I had lost;
I watched the winter gales fade; I saw
    the melting frost.
I dreamed of you whilst duty-bound to
    keep and serve the Law;
My fellow coppers knew my pain, but
    never what I saw;
They brought me lunch and talked to me
    whilst I stared into space,
Beholding you, your fragile lips, your
    fine expressive face;
O fear, ye humans, not to hear and stoop
    to Love's demands,
For he can cut down all your pride, and
    bow you where you stand;
Rietta girl, I should have known far
    better than to think
That you would wait until my heart
    escaped its jailer's clink;
The summer's come whilst you've been
    roaming far from Caledon;

The trees are green, our stream's opaque,
    all life is going on;
My heart is free, and just last week, a
    rose began to grow
In the pot on the balcony beneath my
    flat's window;
I've put a plastic ashtray outside for my
    smoking friends,
But it won't thrive—I'm sure it needs a
    lady's hand to tend—
Eros plays with fire, but will his grace be
    won by rain?
We haven't seen a proper storm since
    last you walked my lane.
There're clouds amassing in the east, and
    when I last looked out,
I saw a slim string of lightning being
    flashed and blown about.
Remember our first kiss?—we were
    standing in the rain,
Outside my flat, and drops were
    splattering against my panes;

We didn't go inside, though we were
both soaked to the bone—
It looks like rain; Rietta girl, when are
you coming home?

LVII

*OH WHAT ARE YOU DOING, AND WHERE
ARE YOU GOING?*

Oh where are you going so far, so far,
  Away from my heart and me?
You are leaving the land where I christened
    your star,
  Where I realized our love could not be.
From the kingdom of woods where the wild
    fairy sleeps,
  Where the fireflies dance in the sky,
You are going—with your footfalls the unicorn
    weeps,
  And the nymph knows her fate is to die.

You have walked on the paths no man's
  footsteps have trod
 Since the age of the dawn of the earth;
Where you stood were felt tremors in tree-root
  and sod
 And the flowers twined out of the turf;
But you came uninvited, and changed
  everything,
 And the flowers felt fairer for you;
And now you are leaving, and what must I sing?
 Will I die like the elven-wood too?

Oh where are you going so far, so far,
 Away from the realm of my love?
With a touch you ignited my helium star,
 With a breath you brought wings to my dove.
In the kingdom of woods where the rainbow sun
  gleams
 Is a bed of leaves dead as my tears,
And your solemn stone bust, which corrodes the
  sunbeams,
 Is the solitary proof of the years;

You won't linger, and why should the woods
    feel the break
  Of the lonely, neglected heart?
You are going—and your footfalls awaken the
    ache
  That your profile, unknowing, did start.
But you came uninvited, and now I am paying
  For a love never borne in your eye;
You talk much to God, but here's everyday
    praying:
  Oh where are you going, and why?

LVIII

AT LAST! A BIT OF PEACE AND QUIET!

At last! a bit of peace and quiet,
    Free from hue and cry;
The flag of Peace I hoist—we fly it,
    Here where heroes lie!

At last! a time of rest and sleeping;
    Drowned, the background noise;
Shut out, the sounds of crying and weeping,
    Silenced, dreadful toys!

At last! the bangs and screams are over;
    Rest our weary heads;
In the still, still day, we under cover
    Crawl back to our beds!

LIX

THE GUARDED HEART

Here, the castle rises,
   Flags and turrets high.
A shadow over it lies,
   And weighs down the eye.
And here, by the mossy stones,
   Here, by the wall,
The guardsmen stand, vigilant,
   Grey-faced and tall.
Guards at the drawbridge;
   Guards in the moat;
Guards on the tower-top,
   In chainmail coats.
Guards in the passages;
   Guards at the gates.
Solemn-faced and sleepless,
   They stand and they wait.
Here, the velvet carpets;
   Here run the stairs,

With crystalline banisters,
   Up into the air.
Here, the highest tower;
   Here, the softest sheets.
Here, the maiden sleeping;
   Amain her heart beats.
Beats all through the evening;
   Beats in the gloom.
Slow heartbeats can be heard
   In the quiet room.
Apart from the beating,
   No sound can be heard;
No song of nightingale,
   No early-morning bird.
So sudden, a ray of light
   Strikes close to the men;
Lights up their gleaming armour,
   Again and again.
No sound from the guardsmen;
   No movement in tow;
But silently, one by one,
   Evaporate like snow.

There's light at the drawbridge;
   There's light in the moat;
Light on the tower-top,
   Where sunrays have smote.
Light in the passages,
   Light on the door.
Light through the window
   And streaming on the floor.
Slowly her smoky eyes
   Are opened by the light,
Slowly she rises
   From years and years' night.
Bare feet on the carpet,
   Bare hands on the door,
The sigh of one expected
   To sleep forevermore.
The drawbridge is open,
   The morning light calls;
Music in the sunshine
   And hymns in the halls.
Music all around her,
   Music in her hair;

Music from the castle,
   And harp-notes in the air.
Prancing in the sunshine
   Like a joyful child,
She steps from the drawbridge
   Out into the wild.
The grasses green velvet,
   The flowers silky red;
A handful of roses
   Creep around in their bed.
In the feral garden
   She is not alone;
One sits, and watches her
   From his golden throne.
Light shines from his profile
   All made up of light;
Seven colours shimmering
   But still purely white.
They're dancing in the garden
   To music in the air,
Dancing with the passion
   That neither can bear;

Dance betwixt the roses,
   Dance the waltz of light;
Dance in each other's arms
   To chase away the night!
The sun it grows hotter,
   The air full of spite;
Pain lances her body
   In fiery flash of light!
She stares at the garden
   Burning away,
And, stumbling on her feet,
   Wails in dismay.
Fire in the garden,
   Fire in his eyes;
Fire all around her,
   Flashing gold sunrise.
Ash from the garden,
   Ash blown by the breeze;
Ash covering the sunlight,
   Halting the disease.
The guardsmen appear again,
   All as before;

All march to the fiery sun
   With challenging roars.
With handfuls of sooty ash
   They drive back the sun,
'Til blessed, cooling darkness
   Has once more begun.
All turn to the maiden,
   Collapsed on the ground;
With worshipful caution,
   They turn her around.
So light on their broad shields,
   They bear her inside;
Once more in the comfy bed,
   Once more in dreams to hide.
Amain, her heart beating,
   Slower than before;
Beating, gently beating,
   It beats forevermore.
Apart from the beating,
   No sound can be heard;
No music in the castle,
   No early-morning bird.

Sleep away the memories;
  Sleep away the pain;
Sleep away all emotion;
  Never wake again!
Here, the maiden lies;
  Here run the stairs,
With crystalline banisters,
  Down from the air.
And here, by the mossy stones,
  Here, by the wall,
The guardsmen stand, vigilant,
  Grey-faced and tall.
Guards at the drawbridge;
  Guards in the moat;
Guards on the tower-top,
  In chainmail coats.
Guards in the passages;
  Guards at the gates.
Solemn-faced and sleepless,
  They stand and they wait.

LX

STORM

What madman's hammer strikes upon
The hallowed realm of Odin's sons?
With every poignant, murderous knell
The skies resound with iron bells.

What sacred fury rends the night
With thrumming strokes of broken light
That claw the sky, to break and smite
The sinful Earth with godly might?

What rage is born of Nature's need
That festers in the hearts of men,
That drives the mind to dastards' deeds,
And hammers in their skulls again?

What cry of fury is it that calls
From all four poles and all four walls,
From ionized air to deluged flame,

And resonates within this brain?

Why, every blow that mighty sword
Rains down upon the peaceful stars,
I shake with rage that heeds no word,
A rage which rattles all the bars

Of all these gates that keep me in—
And, shrieking life, I break and flee
From padded cells of peaceful sin
For stormlands of insanity.

LXI

BUTTERFLY FAR BEYOND WILLOW TREES

Butterfly days by willow trees,
Butterfly days by waterfalls,
Wet by the stream and dried by the breeze;
Butterfly days, when wonder calls—

Butterfly days for young at heart,
Butterfly days for sugar kiss,
To live all the dreams we see in art;
Butterfly days I sorely miss—

Butterfly days! why, I recall
The softness of grass, and the warmth of
    your hand,
Butterfly days! but I did fall
To the hazardous dream of Fantasy-land—

Butterfly days shall be no more,
For like a butterfly in the breeze,
Your soul grew diamond wings, and soared
Like a butterfly, far beyond willow trees.

LXII

O LOVELY ROSE

O lovely Rose, wherefore dost thou not rest?
Wherefore remain awake, unmov'd, unblest,
Clasping the deathly lilies to thy breast
    Beside the window-seat?

Wherefore dost thou not smile when I am near,
As once upon a time thy lips would do?
Wherefore dost thou now shed translucent tears,
Adorn'd in black, who once loved pale blue?

Fair Rose, I miss the lamp-light in thy eyes,
Thy soft lips singing gentle melodies,
Thy fragile namesake dangling gently
    From a slender velvet hand.

Fair Rose, relent! come from that dreary seat,
From where thou watchst the sadly dripping rain;
Come play a game, come laugh, come rest, come eat;

Come speak with me: come ease thy anxious brain!

I'd bring thee all the roses in the land,
If thou would'st just relent! here, take my hand,
And let me near thee without reprimand,
    To take thee in my arms.

I'd bring thee all the roses in the land,
And lay them in a star before thy feet,
Cross glacier-paths, and traverse desert sands,
If it should bring thee comfort on thy seat!

LXIII

THE VAMPYRE QUEEN

A Tale Told in Three Parts

PART I. THE STORY OF HER HISTORY.

The maiden Esriel had been held prisoner
by the cruel Vampyre King, Lanion,

for a hundred years.
How knowledgeable Bards are, I know not,
but whenever they would visit our village
and sing of Esriel,
these are the words they would sing.

    'Now hear my little story,
     Not of war and glory,
  But of great evil and loss.
    The gods did condemn her,
    Put punishment upon her;
Will you hear my tragic story of loss?

'How cold that castle?—No-one knows;
Dark clouds above, dark moor below;
How sad the slaves that all day go
In the great dank dungeon below!
How proud and sad the vampyre-queen
Who casts her gaze upon the green,
Down there, where gravestones silver gleam,
Untouched by moss, the living green.
How dark and cold the tower-room

Where she resides by candle-gloom,
Untouched by drape or gay festoon
To lighten up the deathless gloom!
Nothing to look at, all day long;
Nothing to do but sing a song
That haunts the mountain range along,
And thus she makes her bitter song:
A voice more cruel than witches three,
The slaves below in agony,
A captive ne'er to be set free;
Of this she sings in agony!
By foot of this hill no-one bides
Lest evil things their homes betide;
No creature's seen here, 'less it died
And dragged by wolves the hill beside—
One such there is now, so she sees;
Sinks down upon her ragged knees,
For soon he'll come—this is her geas,
With him, always upon her knees!

'He'll come—he'll come—all in a cloak of mist;
He'll come—he'll come—just let him rob a kiss;

He'll come—he'll come—with speed of thunderbolts;
He'll come—he'll come—before the night is old,
   He'll come with thunderbolts.

  'The rainless moor is gripped with fear,
  The poor slaves huddle there and here;
  Their master comes—they know the tears
  That their queen weeps in grief and fear.
  Through red-rimmed, black-lashed, violet eyes
  She sees her king and knows his guise;
  He once again will take her lies
  And turn them on her cursèd eyes.
  Her blood is his, her life a toy
  For him to maim with hellish joy;
  No maiden more, no virtue coy
  Will save her more against his joy!
  As much a captive as her slaves,
  No fellow-tear her sorrow laves;
  No life has she for death to brave,
  For this she is: his queen, his slave.

'He comes—he comes—beneath a mist of dread;

He comes—he comes—with raging eyes of red;
He comes—he comes—with fire in his hand;
He comes—he comes—with ice upon the land,
  And fire in his hand.

> 'The years slip by without relief;
> The slaves may die—their lives are brief,
> But she lives on: no sneaking thief
> Named Death can bring her soul relief.
> The gods deplore what she has done,
> And so they will not end his fun,
> Nor grant her love from anyone
> But the dark King, who has his fun.
> "Remember your own child," they say;
> "She was born scarce at break of day;
> She loved and trusted all your ways
> Even until her dying day.
> For then, there came a dark-eyed king
> Who took your hand and gave his ring,
> But had no place for children's things—
> What you did then—well, he is *your* king."'

And we knew this was true; for we knew
    the Moor
of Death, as we called it;
and none of us dared to venture upon it.
For evil was upon that moor: deformed
    wolves,
blood-sucking bats, and other such foul
    things.
No-one ever set a toe near it,
except for me.

PART II. THE STORY OF HER HERO.

No-one had mercy upon her;
'Twas right, they said, to suffer thus;
The punishment was not unjust;
Not for a crime done so heinous.
Good people, for a fivescore years
She suffered every whim that he
Would put upon her brutally;
Already dead, was she not free?
  If she wanted, she could go!

I met him, yes, I met the man who tormented his queen;
I saw him first from far away across the cursèd green.
I'd gone to seek a sheep that had gone missing from my flock;
I'd tracked its steps 'til far beyond the limits of my clock.
I was too late—the wolves had long torn its poor life apart;
I watched them slink back to their hill with sad and heavy heart.
As I was turning back to seek the safety of my hut,
A keening noise across the moor did turn my head about.
'I am so close to Deadly Moor,' thought I, now sweating ice,
'That this must be the maid Esriel—I will not venture twice!'
But the sadness and the beauty of that voice across the moor
Did pin me there, although my being all screeched for shelter's door.

I could not leave—she was in pain—my feet were running 'cross
That dreaded moor, where nothing grows save sickly slimy moss.
But then—a shadow overhead—I sprawled upon the ground—
It was darkness all above me, though I could not hear a sound—
In total dread I looked above, and *he* was in the air:
Foul Lanion, and this was more than courage e'er could bear;
In his dark suit he looked no more than any businessman
Such as what haunt the city streets, and cheat you when they can—
But no fat grocer e'er possessed such cloak of smoky mist,
And not even the gravest undertaker has a fist
Made all of iron, wherein he can hold a hand of flame
To lighten up the raven sky—no, Lanion was his name.
Where I lay flat, he did not see, being all intent on
her—

And she was weeping—how she wept! her ailment none
 could cure—
But as fear kept me, moaning softly, on the slimy moss,
I wished that I could get to her, and save her at all cost!
I did not care what she had done—no maid should wail
 so
When her love comes to embrace her—no, kindness she
 should know!
What came across my fevered mind? was it some
 witching-spell
Sent by the maid who cannot die, but lives for e'er in
 Hell?
Who knows?—all I can say is that my haste began to
 cease;
I waited there for seven days, and plotted her release,
And every day I heard her call, as though entreating me
To come with force and brazen will, and bravely set her
 free!
When I awoke the seventh day, my will and heart were
 made;
I set off 'cross that mournful field, bearing my father's
 blade,

Which he had worn in strife and war, to bloody many foes;
That castle seemed to creep on me, that castle no-one knows!
It wasn't long before the wolves came pacing in a pack,
All drooling, snarling, slavering, with jaws and eyelids black;
But slung across my shoulder there was fresh mutton threefold;
I flung the meat away from me—my fear ran rank and cold—
Ignoring me, the greedy wolves attacked the juicy meat;
In haste then I began to move with wings upon my feet;
The dreadful castle towered o'er my frail human will;
I looked up to the turrets bronze, and saw her! maid of ill!
With eyes of gleaming amethyst, long hair of dirty gold,
A spoiled jewel of ancient days, all sparkle now gone cold.
And there I was, thus cowering at dreaded evil's door,
All things to gain, all things to lose, and so I gave a roar
To lift my spirits, quell my fright, and carry me inside

The inner sanctum of the place where dwelt the weeping bride.
No evil waited while I stormed into the entrance-hall,
But, gazing at the spiral stairs that snaked around the wall,
My spirit, for no reason, shrank into the inner deeps
Of human fear, where dreadful gods their silent terror keep.
'Forsooth!' said I; 'Dan Lang, you fool! how many flights of stairs
Have you not braved in all your life, and trod without a care?
And cliffs so steep with jagged rocks you've scaled without a blink;
A flimsy set of spiral stairs: is this what makes you think,
"I cannot do it." Yes, you can! Stop wasting both your eyes;
She waits, and *he*'ll be on his way—Scared shepherd, you must fly!'
I took the step—my feet obeyed the orders of my mind,

And up the stairs I went, and left the entrance hall behind.
But then I felt my dread of it was justified, for there
Most ghastly visions came for me, of creatures from nightmares,
And also things I dreamed and feared when in the darkest night:
My mother's corpse, though she not dead; the wolves o'er it did fight!
And walking dead assailed me, with claws instead of hands;
My sword had no effect, but I then lit a flaming brand;
No creature dared to threaten me as so I went my way
Through the dark land the stairs became, but things I cannot say
What they were, nor how they lived, for they seemed nought but shades,
Crept up on me from every side, darkness and shadow-blades.
Although they could not touch me, I was fearful to touch them,
And so they led me to a marsh, all rot and broken stems

Of long-dead trees, that seemed to writhe across
  towards my feet,
But, *damn this*! I then whirled around, the shades to
  face and beat!
But they had gone!—and right in front of me there was
  a door,
That seemed to beg to open it, for handles there were
  four;
I took my hand and felt the wood: 'twas smoothly sawn,
  and new;
'O Door,' I spoke thus desperately, 'what would you
  have me do?'
A sudden yearning fell on me to open it at once;
I took a handle, began to turn, and stopped—'Are you a
  dunce?
Who knows what lies behind this door?' my conscious
  thoughts did cry,
'It looks so fair, it entreats you—obey it, you will die!'
My hand withdrew, and to my right I spotted a large
  hole,
As deep as Hell, as black as pitch, and fearsome to my
  soul.

'But what,' I fretted, 'is the reason? is this Lanion's spell,
To make the entrance I *should* take seem like the mouth of Hell?
The Door seems fair; the Hole does not; but if this all be lies,
The Hole shall lead me on, and thus by *that* route I must fly!'
No time for doubt—no time to think—I closed my eyes and leapt
Into the blackness, murmuring a prayer that I had kept
For my last seconds, which I feared would soon now be at hand,
And thus I left that magical, and fearful, vampyre-land.

PART III. THE STORY OF HER KING.

>I woke to pain;
>cold stone beneath me, silence beyond me.
>But I had been woken by
>a not disagreeable sensation: a hand sliding
>   up my torso,
>a hand feeling me,

as if to confirm I was there in the flesh.
The hand slid higher—
slender fingers, sharp-nailed,
rested upon my breast. I opened my eyes.

Close to, she was far more repellent, yet far
    more beautiful, than any image my
    mind could have served me.

  Eyes ringed with spiderweb shadows
  In which orbs of dark marble float;
  Pale torn lips stained with scarlet show
A burst of colour on the ashen face and throat.
  Unbrushed and uncared-for, the golden hair
  Still frames her face with softness and grace;
  Features of the girl are corrupted there,
For claws fingernails and fangs teeth replace.
  And from those ravaged lips
  She whispered to me in a fairy's voice;
  Musical and sweet, like an innocent,
As I remained prone, as though I had no choice:

'I know what you seek for, warrior:
To take his own bride from Lanion;
You think you can save her—and you can,
　But not in the way that you would think on.
The maid that inhabited me
Is long gone, yes; long gone;
I am all that remains,
　A shade that continues on.
She refused him many times, so he killed her,
And I, wretched demon, gained a body
　And gave it immortality, so I could live on.
But I bind Lanion eternally,
And keep her soul someplace safe within me,
　So I can continue on.
He keeps his blood in this body,
For bloodless, heartless, lifeless he;
I am his vessel of vitality,
　I live forever, so he can go on.
And I slaughtered the child that she bore,
Saw it die amid squealing and gore,
Threw it to the deformed wolves you abhor,
　And made her continue on.

But the Vampyre King is so tireless
That not even I, a Demon of Wrong,
Can cope with his play, and so I beseech:
   Kill me, and make him forever gone!
The maid that inhabited me
By this deed shall be truly set free;
If you wish her soul with the gods to be,
   Kill me, and make him forever gone!'

But then—

O what have I found, O what have we here?
One who comes to save, a hero without fear?

    She cowered against the battlements like a
       fearful child—

What shall they say of me, what shall they say?
A gallant visited in the middle of the night
   And stole her away?

    Indeed, now it was night:

  We had not heard his flight,
But Lanion now was there, all fangs and mad visage.
   Recovering myself
   I sank my sword in him,
But to no avail: he chuckled at my charge,
   And drew it like a dud,
   Blade innocent of blood,
Unscathed, unharmed, with malice overlarge.

  'Boy, you are weak:
How could you ever think to harm mighty Lanion,
   The destroyer of the meek?

'Have you ever committed a deed so heinous
That you felt it was pure evil?
Have you ever reprimanded yourself
For hurting, maiming, destroying people?
I've always known what I do is wrong
But I've never blamed myself;
All the gods in heaven have taken the blame

For my life and my deeds and my health.
I blend in with the violence, as I cannot bear the silence;
I kidnap all the misfits to make them evil spirits;
I blend in with the violence, the homicidal sequence;
I defile without release, I mingle with the deceased.

'Can you misuse the power of prayer
So as to not heal, but harm?
Have you ever saved one single life
And then wiped out ten more with a swipe of your arm?
I've always known what I do is wrong
But I've never blamed myself;
All the gods in heaven have taken the blame
For my life and my deeds and my health.
I blend in with the violence, as I cannot bear the silence;
I mislead every daughter, I calmly condone slaughter;
I blend in with the violence, the dreaded dirge's cadence;
I haunt the granite tombstones of them who took their own way home.

'And now, boy, do you presume
That this power comes out of nought?
The blood, the life, the world are mine,
A prize for which many of darkness have fought.
I've always known what I do is wrong
But I've never blamed myself;
All the gods in heaven have taken the blame
For my life and my deeds and my health.
I blend in with the violence, as I cannot bear the silence;
The innocents they fear me, no priest dares to come near me;
I blend in with the violence, my putrid breath eloquence,
My schemes of death and suffering, my queen a battered plaything.'

    And thus I understood:
    To remain truly immortal, Lanion
    not only had to drink blood,

but had to transfer his into a living mortal
    with help
from a demon-spell.
But the lady he chose for this task
would not condone it, so in his anger he
    killed her. But
having known her before, the Vampyre
    King
had a hold upon her soul,
and entreated his demon-helper to trap it
and reanimate the body.
Unknowingly, poor Esriel was kept alive,
but the demon controlled her body, and she
    suffered
without hope of deliverance.
But because his blood was in her body,
killing it would kill him,
and set her soul free!
But how could I kill her I had come to save?

The laugh upon his fangs—that evil grin
That spoke to me of malice, lust and sin—

As mighty Lanion thrust a hand of flame,
No noise there was, but silence that appealed to me by name.
    And upon the monster-maiden's face it seemed
    Illusion-light there shined, and Esriel beamed;
    Round-cheeked, blue-eyed, the merry maiden smiled,
And held forth in her pale arms a beautiful ghost-child.
    A blade her breathing chest imbrued with blood,
    And the monster writhed and racked there where she stood.
    And looking down at hands with blood adorned,
I knew the hands were mine, the blade my father's faithful sword.
    Past sound—past words—past me to understand
    The change that befell all of that ghost-land
    As king and lord heaved all his entrails out,
The ripping, shredding roar of an immortal trailed out.
    A pool of blood where Lanion stood dissolved;
    The hungry wail of freed, revengeful souls;
    The shriek of him from afterlife I heard:

The torment he had created now all around him
 burned—
    But my eyes sought only that unliving face,
    Those purple eyes, those shattered lips to trace,
    And there I wept, crouching in all the blood—
I cupped her chin, I stroked her hair, I held her with the
 blood;
    I slowly took from her starved chest the blade
    That cruelly took her cursèd life away;
    Ne'ermore that sword would pierce a living soul,
For where the blade had touched her blood, the iron-
 rust did crawl.
    She moaned—she reached out one sepulchral
 hand
    And called me hero, true-lord of the land,
    As mortal pain my living soul oppressed;
I touched her bloody lips to mine, I clasped her to my
 breast.
    And when my breath had stolen her last cough,
I knew myself for what I was!—I laughed and laughed
 and laughed.

The maiden Esriel was freed.
Her ghost journeyed to the Blessèd Realms,
    there with her babe to be.
And I, deathless become through taking
    breath and blood of a demon,
now drink deep of my glorious immortality.
For I am the true Vampyre King.

LXIV

THE MINES

It's morning now, and soon the sun
Will shine upon the under-tunnelled town:
  A town that's grown, since it begun,
From secret treasure buried fathoms down.
  It's morning now, and soon the sun
Will shine upon the race that rules the mines:
  A race that's learned, since it begun,
All secrets Madame Nature hid with Time.
  'Such cheery fellows!' some will say,

But others think they sing just for relief,
  For through the night 'til dawn of day,
They knock and break the treasure-bearing reef.
    'Come! sing now, Runner, Toby, Jutch;
      Our picks we have for beat;
    And if a rhythm's needed, such
      Create with our feet!
  Rocks! Rocks! Rocks!
    The garnets and metals that gleam,
      The soul of a ring,
      The bane of a king,
    And diamonds are but a dream!'

  They work from dawn 'til dead of night,
Their hands unhurt, their feet still good to go;
  In pockets without candlelight
They know no deep-down fear, nor grief, nor woe.
  They work from dawn 'til dead of night,
Their hands unhurt, their voices never hoarse;
  By campfire or by candlelight
They drive the shadows back with will and force.
  For evermore, they feel the shade

Come creeping from all corners in a cave,
  And fear can only be unmade
By chanting hymns and verses to the brave.
    'Remember Ronnie, Billy, Yort;
      Their ways went down and down;
    The darkness-demon ever sought
      Their lives for his renown.
    Rocks! Rocks! Rocks!
    The crystals that shine in a seam,
      An emerald green,
      The stone of a queen,
    And diamonds we never dream!'

It's evening now, and soon the sun
Will set upon the dusty, draggled town;
  A town with gemstones overrun,
With silver reaped, and copper sulphides sown.
  It's evening now, and soon the sun
Will set upon the ever-bustling mines
  Where ever golden lanterns hung
Keep back the ghosts and shadow-dust of Time.
  'Such cheery fellows!' strangers say;

Who'd ever know they sing just for relief
  Against the dark of night and day,
While 'round them and above them broods the reef.
    'Come! sing of topaz, tiger's eye;
      Thrice merry men are we,
    For all the wealth we could desire
      Is here for us to see.
Rocks! Rocks! Rocks!
The stone with a cold-bitter gleam,
    The prize of the land,
    The blood of our hands;
The diamond of all our dreams!'

LXV

THE PEOPLE

We lay here, unbeknown and yet untold,
A mighty host in waiting for the tomb,
And nothing fills this monstrous, empty room,
    But silence—and the cold.

We lay here, unbeknown and yet untold,
And all around us is the stench of death;
What air we have, belabours our breath,
    And welcomes in the cold.

We lay here, unbeknown and harmless, now,
When once they feared our rage and our spears;
When once, hunger and pain were not *our* fears,
    Not ours to feel or know.

We lay here, unbeknown and harmless, now,
A thousand warriors' corpses underfoot;

A strong young voice now old and cracked and mute;
    In dust you see us bow.

We lay here, unbeknown and yet untold,
Nursing the septic wounds of our hate;
We have seen fall of many who were great,
    And melting of so much gold.

We lay here, unbeknown and yet untold,
With nothing now to steal the pain away;
We did the deeds: we fought, we took our pay:
    Bright guns for our gold.

While diamonds still sparkle in the sun,
While ravaged forests smoulder in their hearts,
While lions feed on those we ripped apart,
    Our era here—is done.

As deserts over ruined pastures run,
As every trace of inhumanity
Is scoured from here with sand and shrub and tree,
    Our lifetime here is done.

LXVI

A HAIR

    One day, when you no longer call me fair;
When all our long love and passion have died,
And both of us fairly indemnified;
    When in your house my face is found nowhere,
One day, mayhap, you'll turn the TV on
And dig amongst the cushions for change gone
    Into the fetid couch's spongey care;
And there, with wraps of chips both old and new,
Dust particles, dog-hairs and teaspoons, you
    Mark one gold hair.

    When I no longer keep your heart from wear,
New faces will appear to staunch the flood,

The mess I left: salt tears, life-giving blood
    You'll cry, and my soft shoulder won't
be there.
Mayhap your ornaments a fairer eye
Will view, but hastily you'll push her by
    The tank of little fishes in your care,
For near their filter, snaked along the glass,
Too pale to mistake, too cruel to pass,
    Sticks one gold hair.

    To forget me, you will have to prepare:
Shatter the frames I made of me and you,
Throw out the cotton sheets I bought brand-
new,
    Abolish every dish we used to share.
But if, one day, your loose-paged study guide
Slides down between the wall and the
bedside,
    In vain will be all your painstaking care.
For as you crawl beneath your bed, your arm
Disturbs the dust that kept so long from harm
    One golden hair.

    And so, my love, my heart's primary
care,
Forget not this, forget not me, but keep
In all your ways, awake or fast asleep,
    Intact the knowledge pure of what we
share,
For ever part of me will haunt your rooms,
The part untouched by brushes, pans or
    brooms,
    And will not leave with me, no matter
where.
Swear to me, love, that always in your soul
You'll keep pristine, untarnished, beautiful,
    One golden hair.

LXVII

BLUE NATION

I rolled out of bed in the morning,
Flung open my closet wide;
Today is the day that I wear my blue dress
And throw my grey trousers aside.
But my roommate looked at me with eyes so
  wide;
Said, 'You're not wearing blue,
Are you?
Everyone knows that green is the shade
That everyone's wearing!' And so she laid
Out for me a green skirt, green blouse, green
  shoes;
And so I, not wanting to be awfully rude,
Dressed in that green skirt, green blouse, green
  shoes,
And went out to look for you.

All day long across the classroom I faced
Your friends, arrayed all in red;
With your red suit and shoes, you were perfectly
    placed;
Not a hair was astray on your head.
And I? Oh, I yearned to go over to you,
And but for the gulf between,
The gulf that separated red and green,
I would have gone over to you.

But as you left you brushed past my place,
And one of your eyes caught mine;
Your outstretched hand was on my green
    pencil-case;
I looked down and murmured: 'Just leave. I'm
    fine.'

I sat in my room for an hour apace,
With my green sleeve rolled up on my wrist,
But however hard I tried, I could not discard
    your face,
The red one I had lately kissed.

I will make a decision: am I red or green?
Which colour is on me most comely to be seen?
Now I wish I could keep the assurance of the
    grey
And never have to be red or green.

Today, when I awoke, my blue dress was lying
All crumpled, on my bedroom floor;
I lifted it slowly, didn't notice I was crying,
And flew out of the dormitory door.

And when I saw you in those blue, blue trousers
    and shirt,
The shade that suits you, love, the best,
I danced up to you, matching trouser to skirt—
Let them judge—we are not like the rest!

LXVIII

SISTER SOFTLY SLEEPING

Will you shout *now*, when they lay her down in limp
    redundancy?
    She, who never cried before—
Do you think you know the secrets that she whispered
    to the night
    From that uncorrupted core—
Do you know with all your heart that what she said and
    did was right?
    The twilight now is deepening
      And the wilting roses fall;
      Still beneath their petals' pall
    Lies our sister, softly sleeping.

Will you shout *now*, now that those who jeered and
    slanderized her faith
    Lay her gentle head to rest;
When the zealots that condemned her speak of sweet
    holistic gain—

Call her peaceful, call her blessed?
She shared no peace, no brotherhood, with them who forge the chains.
    In the midnight darkly deepening
      An angel made a light,
      But she succumbed to a blight,
      And now she lies here, softly sleeping.

Will you shout *now*, when the cause she fought for deep inside the earth
    Lies as gas, evaporates?
Now you see her pain: it rises, oh! we cower from its face.
    Sit you silent, sit and wait
For a day when God provides all love, all justice, all His grace.
    Touch her beauty; now it's deepening,
      Deeper now than ever before,
      Safe behind this dreaded door
      With our sister, softly sleeping.

Will you shout *now*, when the turncoats all have found their rich release?
    Hear them say: 'Our voice is dead;
You know, she only thought of struggle: let us find an easy road.
    Even if we must share a bed
With those we counted our tyrants, we cannot embrace her load.'
    Lady Freedom now is weeping,
      Not for death so sad and wane,
      But for the immortal pain
    Of our sister softly sleeping.

Will you shout *now*? did you love her? do you love her like I do?
    Will you stand at arms with me
For her sake, for all the love she bore her life, her land, for you?
    I shall never flag nor flee:
Are you with me? have you decided? would you die for freedom, too?
    Look, the turncoats now are weeping:

>How they lie! they know no pain;
>   Their filthy hands profane
>Our lovely sister, softly sleeping.

Am I crying *now*? will my heart break? I have never shed a tear,
   No matter what went wrong;
She was my comfort, when she held me—oh, I needed nothing more—
   So beautiful, brave and strong,
She was a presence that no-one could ever waiver or ignore.
>   In this chaos wildly leaping
>   We cannot right the wrongs,
>   We cannot stand so strong
>   As our sister softly sleeping.

Do you think that, if we died here, if we slew all who betrayed,
   And after death we saw her soul,
She might forgive us all, the true and false alike, and be content?

Oh, she offered me this role:
Role of captain in her stead, but how?—my will and
heart are bent!
    The darkness now is deepening,
      For my feeble heart is broken
      By that gentle request spoken
    By our sister softly sleeping.

You're right, of course: she'll not forgive our deaths
right here and now:
    We've got to forage on,
Make her proud, so when we meet her, we can hold
heads high and smile.
    The weak at least are gone:
Those who doubted, did not love her: they have joined
our lords so vile.
    For them will be no weeping,
      No matter what befall:
      They betrayed the hope, the call
    Of our sister softly sleeping.

Will you come now? I am sorry that I ever doubted you;
    Come fight with me for hope;
Let the memory of our sister be a living, burning flag
    That we carry up this slope,
Leading a generation that will rise out of their rags.
    O! this artificial weeping
      Will be thoroughly unmade,
      And the proper honour paid
    To our sister softly sleeping.
    Someday soon, instead of weeping,
    We will lay down, sweetly sleeping.

LXIX

CALL TO TROY

Come with us to fight:
For every sword and every godly hand,
The steeds of iron stamping in the sand,
All quaking with anticipation stand,
    Awaiting triumph of right.

Come with us to glory:
Immortal heroes line up one by one,
Bright spears and breastplates gleaming in the sun,
From which the foe—the cowards—soon shall run,
    And we shall be the victors of the story.

Come with us to war:
Our hosts will overrun the countryside;
On beasts with flaming nostrils we will ride,
And every man will know: they cannot hide
    From our divine law.

Come with us to death:
For sweet and glorious is the ferry-ride
Leading fallen heroes to the other side,
Where those beloved of nymphs and gods reside,
    Exchanging immortality for death!

LXX

THE LAMENT OF THE ELVES FOR THEIR DEAD WARRIORS

Who knows what lies beyond
these gaping doors of Death?
None but the dead can tell.

Enter you, the maiden with the love-curse upon
    your breast;
enter you, the stillborn infant;
enter you, the man of dignified age;
though death has divided you,

the matron of your heart waits to welcome you
    inside.
Enter you, the laughing child prematurely invited;
your happy presence cheers this hall of gloominess.
Enter you, dripping wounds of filthy Murder;
enter you, crushed under the designs of Fate;
enter, peasant; and enter, lord;
enter, harlot and queen;
enter, children of the weary world.

Who knows what lies beyond
these gaping doors of Death?
None but the dead can tell.

Now enter you, soldier;
you who died swiftly under the stroke of the
    painless sword;
you who perished in agony beneath the smoke of
    the battlefield;
you who died not upon the field of blood,
but suffered an ignoble, festering death upon the
    sick-benches.

Enter, soldiers,
you who were ravished in the streets of victory;
you, cut down as you attempted to flee.
Enter, soldiers;
behind these dark doors strife ceases to exist.
Enter, soldiers;
lay down your heavy heads; there is now no
    obstacle before your rest.

Who knows what lies beyond
these gaping doors of Death?
None but the soldier can tell.

LXXI

THE WINNER

> *'You're not gonna lose me, Matilda.*
> *You've given me a taste for life.*
> *I'm gonna be happy, sleep in a bed, have roots—*
> *And never be alone again, Matilda.'*
> —Léon, *The Professional* (1994)

What have I not endured,
In what currency have I not paid the price?
    You sat and never stirred,
And all you had to offer was more vice.
Two gunshots at the door of Fate, the toll you
    pay for death;
The price for me to curse you more with every
    waking breath;
    You won the game, my love:
Your blackened heart moved me to lighten
    mine,
    Placing innocence above
My survival: love, stay innocent, stay mine.

    To touch your heart and hands,
To throw away all thought of right and wrong—
    Unthinkable demands
You make of me: can I resist for long?
Kill for money, kill for you; until we both are stained with blood;
Will we never walk away? will we not cower before God?
    You have won the game, my love:
I fight no more the chaos that you bring,
    But leave innocence above
The wounds imposed by every worldly thing.

    But to see you dying here,
Taking everything away from me tonight,
    Is one scene I won't endure;
I will plunge myself in you, and end the fight.
    I will kill to preserve you,
All your vices, all your virtues, every breath;
    I will make a life with you,

Where the air we breathe has got no stench of death.
You have perpetrated all your fear and horror into me;
I have no defences left and no desire to be free.
    You won the game, my love:
I keep you with me till the day I die;
    I will make a life of love
With you, and never live another lie.

LXXII

WEREWOLF SONG: NIGHTSHADE AND HARP

The sunlight is waning, but darkness is slow,
And the queen of the sky has a long way to go.
The full moon is weeping; the rain is her tears;
She hunts in the dark through the cycle of years.
Come wake from your cage, love, and hearken to me;
Come waken the woodlands from complacency;
The earth is below us, the full moon above,

And the earth and the moon shall approve our love.
The sunlight is waning, though darkness is slow,
And the harsh gritty earth starts to soften and glow.
Take my feet and my hands and dredge me from the deep;
Come with nightshade and harp; come and sing me to sleep.

To the tree in the woods that both lives and is dead,
Where the bright wanton moon makes her nuptial bed,
Where the earth is relieved of his mundanity,
There I lie: wake, my love, and come hearken to me.
The moon laughs through her tears and shakes out her hair,
Sheds a silvery light that the earth takes to bear.
Twelve nights in the year they are met face to face;
For twelve nights in the year they can touch and embrace.
To the tree in the woods that both lives and is dead,
Come hearken to me, to our nuptial bed.

Take my feet and my hands and dredge me from the deep;
Come with nightshade and harp; come and sing me to sleep.

For the night is but short, and the light days are long,
And I wither and weep when you silence your song;
For the earth shall withdraw from the wistful moon,
And his consort, the sun, shall awaken him soon.
With half an eye open the moon shall arise,
And she contents herself with the court of the skies.
The selfish earth stirs to the stroke of the sun;
Withdraw again, love, for the day has begun.
   For the night is but short, and the daytimes are long,
   And a month shall elapse before our next song;
   Take my feet and my hands and dredge me from the deep;
   Come with nightshade and harp; come and sing me to sleep.

LXXIII

CLAWS

Skali's a kitten with terrible claws,
A soft tabby kitten with cotton-white paws.
Skali's a demon who delights to draw
Blood with her spiky and scissor-sharp claws.
Sweet tabby kitten slinks in at the door,
Sweet tabby kitten rolls round on the floor.
Feel with a foot for the cat on the floor,
She sinks in her teeth and her fangs and her claws.
Now you know that a tomcat is stubborn and set;
When a tom has a queen on his tiny mind set,
His fleas and his faith, all furore he forgets.
Well, she rolled and she purred and she acted a pet—
The large ginger tom sat and watched this coquette;
They purred a most pleasing and profound duet.
He thought he had conquered this pleasing coquette,
But in claiming his prize, he too soon did forget
Of all things but the joy he was going to get,
And in coming too close, was caught fast in her net.

Out came the claws of the conquered coquette!
No, his wails of woe we shan't soon forget!
Skali's a kitten with milky-white paws,
A soft ball of fluffy with needlelike claws.
Skali's a lady who'll lay on the floor,
Tempting a lover with lily-white paws.
O tomcats, beware of those terrible claws;
Beware of those wiles from the queens you adore,
For it's pain to get caught and scratched by those claws,
By the siren with snowy and silky-soft paws.

LXXIV

REASONS YOU SHOULDN'T LEAVE

You sleep like the dead
on our shared bed of chaos and disorder;
are you drunk—or are you dying—are you
    contemplating murder?
If it's murder, murder me:
kill the one who fears to love, but not to die,

who will use you if you let me.
But you won't—

You'll let those others enter, but not me:
not me—for fear I change you, heal your
    promiscuity,
or for fear I'll be myself, and you'll be
just another notch on my bedpost,
another mark on my headboard,
another bloodstain on my carpet,
for you know me.

Sleep well, but not too long;
for the icy axeman comes,
and the deathwatch beetle chirps,
and the day is nearly done.
On the far-off ridge of the world the dawn
    stands pale and dead
and the stars fly heedless in their spheres like
    the virtue that has fled
from you, from you and me;

we have given up our treasures to war and
    diplomacy.
The blood that we have spilt together will
    become a raging sea.

We had joy together, once:
when we each thought of the other
not as bedmates, but a sister and her brother;
but the velvet rose blooms red,
and the swollen grapes grow red,
and the mist in my eyes is red,
and the hellish scarlet lust lies on us both,
as the guilty moonlight swathes our shared
    incestuous bed.

I want so hard to forget—
Please come away with me,
for you sleep sound like the dead,
like those that die in space,
with no sound of catastrophe;
only suffocating nothingness,
floating for eternity.

I never want to forget—
If you've any heart, you won't leave me;
for you're more than just a bloodstain:
you are fire, you are life,
you're the source of all my pain,
the rage that drives my knife,
the heat that suffuses my brain.

Halina—goddess—Harley Simpson—you are
    terrible as life,
as cold as the bringer of death,
as intoxicating as absinthe breath,
as warm and wet as the fleeting one-night wife.
I ache for you in my entirety;
come rescue me from drowning in this scarlet,
    frothing sea;
lave me with those swollen lips,
and the velvet touch of your fingertips;
let me move again inside you;
let me sleep, but not to dream;
cut off from war, from power—from my
    nightmares, from the screams—

curled carelessly together
with the softness, with the pleasure, and my
    dreams—

Now I go, and do not ask
for any reply from you:
if you can sleep, and sleep like the dead,
I never wish to wake you,
but I go,
I go to search for some cheap distraction to
    replace you.

LXXV

FAREWELL

Go, she said, *go sing those songs for both of us.*
As that soul I held immortal
fluttered dying on its way
she held me fast and said again:
Go, beloved, go.

I shut my eyes and shook my head:
Let's meet our doom together.
Surely without you I will fill the world with screams,
and my songs will all be of death.
Let me remain
a phantom beside you, ever longing,
calling forth from my harp those days
when we two roamed the boundless world together
and lingered in those valleys filled with music
that resounded to the choir of eldritch voices,
the hymns of the race immortal.
I will hover here by you, a restless spirit,

and sing of sunny days
before the darkness,
and that quest which stained our happiness for ever.

Yet her eyes, for she could no longer speak, implored
    me.
And so I left.
Go, she said, *go sing those songs for both of us.*
I wiped her bloody lips, I closed her eyes,
pressed against her for one last dear kiss,
and left her there in the land of horror.

LXXVI

THE NIGHT IS BEAUTIFUL

    The night is beautiful,
Cool purple blackness to douse ourselves in.
    The night is beautiful,
Soft moonshine glow tempering the bright city lights.
    The night is so beautiful
That even the rampaging dawn hesitates to ravage her.

LXXVII

PEGGY MAY OF THE NORTH COUNTRY

O young Peggy May were a lass fair an' fey
Fro' the cold wintry wolds o' the North Country;
Strung she sair like a Muse on her harp e'ery day,
Fa' her kin had all gone an' been drowned in the sea.

Said the fair Peggy May one bra' summer's day:
'O! respite me fro' mine an' me own misery!
Wi' these braw buckled schoon I sa' fly far away,
An' ne'er more be seen in the North Country.

'Where the smooth summer streamlets go sailin' down,
By the wide wand'ring walls o' fair London-town;
Where the green fields among the straight stream flie'th
    along,
Sa' I take there my harp and abide ay in song.'

So she set down the road tae the South Country,
Peggy May by the streams leadin' down tae the sea.

An' she lacked ne'er fa' victual, nor hosen an' schoon,
Fa' the spell o' her harp by the charm o' the moon.

One fa' the leman an' one fa' the maid!
An' one fa' the orphan who laugh'd as she play'd!
An' mony a gentleman smil'd but to see
Such a fair bonny lass in the South Country!

'O fair Peggy May, by my silver an' gold,
By the corn in my fields an' the kine in my fold,
I sa' build thee a keep in yon mountains tae dwell,
In the wild ebon crags 'twixt the dales an' the dells.'

'O gentleman ony, tho' he claim'th so much ground,
Canna cage me, fa' I hight Peggy May;
An' high in the cold crags, O the walls wend around,
An' I ne'er sa' see 'gin the light o' the day.'

'By the songs that I sing, an' the valleys that hear,
An' the calm blue waters in the heart o' the mere,
I sa' array thee in apparel fresh fro' the spring,
An' thou sa' be my shepherdess wi' me tae sing.'

'Nae changelin' be I, tae be decked ay in bloom,
An' nae nymph I be, fa' I hight Peggy May:
Return, piping shepherd, tae yon lamb an' yon loom:
Ah they yearn ay fa' ye, an' entreat ye tae stay.'

'By the height o' my helm, an' the steel o' my sword;
By the shriek o' my trumpet, the weight o' my word;
But bequeath tae me justly the gift o' thy name,
An' thou sa' hight a lady o' knightly fame.'

'Tho' be ye sae stern an' sae strong an' sae tall,
I should be ay a lily on leathern tae lay.
Fro' the rump o' yon destrier I sure be tae fall:
Nanesuch flower be I, fa' I hight Peggy May.'

One fa' the leman an' one fa' the maid!
An' one fa' the orphan who laugh'd as she play'd!
An' mony a gentleman wept but tae see
Such a free comely lass in the South Country!

So made she ay merrily tae great London-town,
Where the smooth summer streamlets go sailin' down,
An' the broad bustlin' streets be all paven wi' gold,
Where the soft city air maketh man an' maid bold.

One fa' the leman an' one fa' the maid!
An' one fa' the orphan who laugh'd as she play'd!
Sae the fair Peggy May synde in great London-town
When the wild winter waters kam a-wailin' down.

O! young Peggy May, we be all woe an' wae,
Since the bra' summer's day thou wendest away;
Thou recall'st ay the bustle o' braw London-town
While the wild winter waters went a-wailin' down.

Ye sa' see the maiden wi' harp ne'ermore,
Since she, singin,' went ay oh so far fro' the shore;
An' the wild winter waters wept thunder that day,
An' that was the end o' fair Peggy May.

One fa' the leman an' one fa' the maid!
An' one fa' the orphan who laugh'd as she play'd!

Oh, mony a gentleman smil'd but to see
Such a rare bonny lass in the South Country!

O! fair Peggy May, thou sa' haunt the fair day,
By the white o' the waves an' their boom in the bay;
Thou sa' sail wi' thy kin o'er the endless sea,
Fro' the cold wintry wolds o' the North Country!

LXXVIII

FROZEN ROAD

The city wakening as I walk,
Through gates and roads I make my way.
My boots are firm upon my path;
My weary feet must still go on.
I've set that flimsy bridge alight;
I've left for good that hallowed ground;
The flames burn there forevermore,
But now I turn into the mist.
I saw you on the other side,

But now you've gone so far away;
In order to return to me,
You've got to let me go.

Where ravens fly, I wend my way,
And through the mists the towers rise;
I hesitate, to stay with you,
But plunge into the mist again.
The ravens call from tops of trees;
I wind my way into the woods;
The silence falls, the mist recedes,
And for a moment all is peace.
But flickering lights bewilder me;
The cold springs up to lick my face;
On farther paths, in denser woods,
I'm doomed to wander, still alone.
You'll save me not with shining sun;
Leave back your dreams of summertime,
But, frozen heart to frozen heart,
You have to let me go.

I cannot leave the winter woods—
Not while the ravens call to me—
My weary feet will ever tread
The road my mind has journeyed on.
I seek to find something to seek;
I seek to loosen tangled bonds;
If I choose to untangle you,
Will you still follow, close to me?
Your path and mine may never meet,
But if you follow through the mist,
Boot-prints, dead leaves, a frozen road:
You've got to let me go.

LXXIX

FAIR ARE THE BRIDES

'O fair are the brides o' the country,
    An' fair are the brides o' the Hall,
But the brides that syne in old Troya town
    Are the fairest o' them all.'

The king ower the sea
    Proclaimeth in royaltie:
'I gae tae win an' tae bring her back hame,
    The fairest o' all ladie.'

But she kam nae unto him;
    She kam nae ower the sea;
She hath scorned his gold an' his jewels sae bright,
    An' remaineth in libertie.

Fast fifty thousand men o' the West,
    Sae bold an' sae bra' an' tall,
Kam tae win an' tae bring her back hame,

    The fairest bride o' them all.

But she kam nae unto them;
    She kam nae ower the sea,
She hath scorned their arms an' their swords sae red,
    An' remaineth in libertie.

    Murther by house an' hall,
        Black winds upon the sea,
An' a' fa' the sake o' that woman sae proud,
        The fairest o' all ladie.

The prince o' the golden hall
    Gaeth tae ask o' the fair ladie:
'O fa' what syne ye here, an' gae ne nae
    Tae thy true-love ower the sea?'

'O my true-love I hath nae seen,
    Nae seen by the golden hall,
Fa' he gaeth ae in wisdom, an' heedeth nae fool,
    The lightest brow o' them all.'

The fals knight o' the Lilie
    Gaeth tae ask o' the fair ladie:
'O fa' what shew yer tears, an' gae ne nae
    Tae thy true-love ower the sea?'

'O my true-love I hath nae seen,
    Nae seen by the lilie hall,
Fa' he falleth nae by field or by flood,
    The firmest arm o' them all.'

The fals bishop o' the sea-god's hall
    Gaeth tae ask o' the fair ladie:
'O fa' what shew yer pride, an' gae ne nae
    Tae thy true-love ower the sea?'

'O my true-love I hath nae seen,
    Nae seen by the sea-god's hall,
Fa' his bearin' is stark, an' his brow made o' flame,
    The proudest wight o' them all.'

She kam nae unto him,
    The fairest o' a' ladie;

She lieth sae still, an' loveth ne nae,
    Beside the frothin' sea.

The good knights o' Troya town
    Are red as red can be,
An' they lift ne their limbs, an' hear nae mair
    The cries o' the fair ladie.

Fa' he kam there unto her,
    The king ower the sea,
Where nae still bideth tae shield her still,
    The fairest o' a' ladie.

The prince o' the golden hall
    Lieth dead as dead can be,
An' a' fa' the sake o' the red, red gold,
    An' the groom o' royaltie.

The fals knight o' the Lilie
    Ne nae sa' buried be,
Fa' the sake o' the folk o' fair Troya town,
    An' the fairest o' all ladie.

The fals bishop o' the sea-god's hall
    In Heaven we sa' ne see,
Fa' the sake o' the hand o' that ladie bright,
    An' the weepin' o' maidens tae see.

But she kam nae unto him,
    The king ower the sea,
Fa' he's back tae the west wi' his swords sae red,
    An' bideth there in crueltie.

LXXX

IN THE CITY WHERE THE RAIN STILL FALLS

In places where the rain still falls
There are secrets and sacred ways;
There is a shadow that beckons,
At the same time, pushing back.
There is a goddess who walks
Barefoot on the hidden paths,

And over her shoulder the shadow calls,
In places where the rain still falls.

   Child of the youngest city,
   Born of the deepest shadow,
   Will I follow her forever,
Even as she is lost from my sight?
   I see a twisting alleyway,
   And a path to the home of my youth,
And a shadow over the stony halls
In places where the rain still falls.

   The rain washes away my fever
   As I wander through the unknown,
   Ever thinking, never concluding,
Soft raindrops over these streets of stone.
   Faces of people, further away,
   And a home in the halls of a heart,
And a faraway voice which softly calls,
In this city where the rain still falls.

LXXXI

ELDERTREE

The leaves are falling in Eldertree,
Where once the king kept company
In days when all the folk were free,
In days when you were here with me.
Golden leaves now falling free:
It sears my heart, it comforts me,
  This wind from out the north.

The leaves are fallen in Eldertree,
Where now I find no company.
The woods and fields are wild and free,
But none are here to walk with me.
Golden leaves have fallen free;
Be still, my heart, and comfort me,
  Thou wind from out the north.

LXXXII

WINTERAAND OP DIE HOËVELD

Blou donker omsluit my; ek is alleen.
Dog nie alleen, nooit.
Die wêrelde ontmoet mekaar, deurdring mekaar.
Die maan word 'n koue elektriese brand.
Elke stêr in die hemel gloei met warm heksevuur.

Ek is alleen, omring deur krakende doringbome.
Swart assegaaie word om my gehef, elke doring 'n punt
  van staal.
Dolke vir die maan se bloed.
Koue assegaaie drink die warm bloed van die sterre.
'n Skadu van ys trek deur my lyf.

Ek is alleen, en klein voor die gevaar.
Elke bosritsel word die gegrom van 'n Hoëveld heks.
Elke bewegende skadu is die swart-bekolde jagter.
Sy sluip geruisloos in die koue kuss van die maan.
Vurige oë weergee die gloed van 'n verre stêr.

Sy is alleen.
Oor die droë veld ruis die stilte van groot geheimnisse.
Ons struikel oor die lewelose gras met bebloede knieë,
met die ysterpunte van swart assegaaie gerig op ons rûe.
Ons volg die maan.

—

WINTER'S NIGHT ON THE HIGHVELD

I am alone, blue darkness enfolding me.
Yet not alone, never.
The worlds touch; each passes through the other.
The moon is a cold blue ball of light.
Every star in the sky glows with burning witchfire.

I am alone, surrounded by the creak of thorn-trees.
Black spears surround me, a tip of steel surmounting
    every thorn.
Daggers for the blood of the moon.
Cold spears drink the hot blood of the stars.
A shadow of ice passes through my body.

I am alone, and tiny before the danger.
A witch's mutter sounds in the rustling of every bush.
The spotted hunter moves in every shadow.
In the cold kiss of the moon she slinks silently,
her fiery gaze reflecting the glow of a distant star.

She is alone.
The silence of great secrets susurrates over the dry
    grasses.
Through the lifeless grass we stumble, bloodying our
    knees,
steel spear-points aimed at our backs.
We follow the moon.

LXXXIII

THE VISITOR

I come.
I sneak into the city on quiet feet.
I press my cold face up against the colder
 window-glass.
I feel the warmth inside those rooms and I
 recoil.
 The city is mine.
I go padding down the silent streets and caress
 the empty cars.
The midnight stars watch me.
I hover at the space between earth and sky.
My tears trickle from the gutter and feed the
 watching moss.
I breathe through the ghost fingers of one
 wavering hand.
 I move slowly.
I embrace the darkness of the waiting graveyard.
I clasp my cloying hands around the late-night
 onlooker.

I hide the stars away.
I spread the silence thickly over my entire
  domain.
I murmur along the railroad and lie in wait
  under the bridge.
I dim the street-lamp and muffle the growl of
  the oncoming truck.
I dampen laughter, conceal danger, and brood
  over the sleeping city.
I have consumed everything.
  Dawn comes.
I fling my arms wide to embrace the steely
  winter sun.
  I die.

LXXXIV

THE YEARS

I wrote a thousand poems of love,
   Not one of them for you—
A thousand words I longed to hear
   But none of them from you.
With fantasies I made my days
   Seem bearable and full;
A thousand loves my dreams gave me,
   But none of them were you.

I had a thousand lustful thoughts,
   Not one of them for you;
I ruined my youth in dreary dreams,
   But never thought of you.
The sun was cruel; the moon was cold,
   The days passed day by day,
And though the deepest realms I searched,
   I never did find you.

I wept a thousand lonely tears,
    Not one of them for you;
With broken heart I looked for you
    Throughout the empty world.
And all I found were my own tears;
    They never could find you,
And, unfulfilled, I made a path
    That led away from you.

I found a lonely place to wait,
    And there I made my home;
And dozens came upon that place,
    But none of them were you.
I braced myself to endure love
    With one who was not you;
I sat and waited long for you,
    But still, you never came.

I waited until surely I
    Was far too old for you;
My hair was moss, my skin was stone,
    So well hidden from you.

And when you came upon me there,
   I would not wake for you;
I knew, with all my beauty gone,
   I was no mate for you.

But there you stood, and never left,
   And now I can see you,
And there you raised your hand to touch,
   To show the way to you.
And here my skin all made of stone
   Longs for nothing but you,
And here my crumbling, dying heart
   Keeps pace in tune with you.

But how can I believe it's real
   When I am holding you?
And how can I believe the years
   Have not ruined me for you?
The years seem now like loyal friends,
   When they have made me wise,
But how can I believe that you
   Would touch me, would love me?

A thousand words I heard from you
    To make me wise and strong;
A thousand smiles you've given me
    And all of them for you.
And when I read those poems now,
    I know one constant truth:
In dream, in thought, in word and deed,
    They were, truly, all for you.

CREDITED ILLUSTRATIONS

Page 12: From a drawing in 'Songs For Little People,' Norman Gale, 1896.

Page 13: From 'Scan This Book,' compiled by John Mendenhall.

Page 17: From a drawing in 'Illustreret Danmarkshistorie For Folket,' Adam Fabricius, 1854.

Page 39: From a drawing in 'The Domestic Cat: Bird killer, mouser and destroyer of wild life; means of utilizing and controlling it,' Edward Forbush, 1916.

Page 40: From 'The Story of Our Merchant Marine,' by Willis J. Abbot, 1919.

Page 44 and 46: From 'The Bride's Cook Book,' 1912.

Page 81 and 84: 'Fern Leaf Silhouette' by Karen Arnold.

Page 89: From 'Holiday Plays For Home, School and Settlement,' by Virginia Olcott, 1925.

Page 91: From a drawing by Charles Lebrun published in 'L'Encyclopédie ou Dictionnaire Raisonné des

Sciences, des Arts et des Métiers,' by Diderot and D'alembert (1751; 1772).

Page 101: From a drawing in 'Az Osztrák-Magy ar Monarchia Irásban és Képben,' 1885.

Page 104: From a drawing in 'Lullabies of Many Lands Collected and Rendered Into English Verse,' Alma Strettell, 1894.

Page 111: From 'Drinks of the World,' by James Mew and John Ashton, 1892.

Page 119: From the archives of Pearson Scott Foresman, donated to the Wikimedia Foundation.

Page 120: Traced from 1908 Sears, Roebuck Catalogue

Page 121: From a drawing in 'Le Monde Vu par les Artistes,' Rene Menard, 1881.

Page 200: From 'Line and Form,' by Walter Crane, 1914.

Page 209: From the archives of Pearson Scott Foresman, donated to the Wikimedia Foundation.

Page 224: From a drawing by Marie L. Danforth in 'Short Stories For Short People,' by Alicia Aspinwall, 1896.

Page 234: From the archive of Pearson Scott Foresman, donated to the Wikimedia Foundation.

Page 240: From 'Eros and Psyche: A Fairy-Tale of Ancient Greece Retold After Apuleius,' by Paul Carus, 1900.

www.ingramcontent.com/pod-product-compliance
Lightning Source LLC
Chambersburg PA
CBHW022047290426
44109CB00014B/1016